The Global Stock Market Nexus Considering External Factors

Dong Xiyong

Paths International Ltd

中国财经出版传媒集团
中国财政经济出版社

Preface

This thesis provides three empirical essays on the global stock market nexus considering external factors. The first essay explores the global economic factors that significantly impact on emerging Asian stock market returns, and especially those that were important during the financial crisis, by applying a dynamic model averaging (DMA) approach. Due to marketization and globalization, emerging Asian stock markets are influenced by numerous global factors, such as the business cycle, uncertainty in economic and monetary policy, financial and commodity markets, and investor sentiment. Moreover, the advantage of DMA approach is that it takes account of the fact that forecasting models and their coefficients can change over time. However, unlike existing DMA studies that consider only forecasted asset prices, we analyse both the in-sample relationship and out-of-sample predictability of the impact of global factors on stock returns, according to the sensitivity of stock markets. In terms of in-sample relationship, we find that developed stock and exchange rate markets show a strong relationship with emerging Asian stock markets due to financial market integration. In contrast, the forecasting power of economic fundamentals is highest out-of-sample because stock markets reflect real economic activity.

The second essay examines the potential influence of exogenous shocks on time-varying correlations and portfolio strategies between the emerging Asian and other global stock markets. Using the ARMA-cDCC-FIEGARCH model with and without exogenous shocks, we find the shocks from the U. S. stock market have a greater influence on global stock markets compared to that from U. S. economic policy. Fortunately, the model with exogenous shocks improves its accuracy, which plays the same role of controlling structural breaks in the model. More importantly, incorporating exogenous shocks in our model also provides better value at risk performance results and hedging effectiveness. Moreover, our results highlight the usefulness of including other global stock assets in the traditional portfolio for emerging Asian market investors. However, investors have limited opportunities to diversify their assets during the global financial crisis.

The third essay investigates the dependence structures for six regional stock markets according to different market conditions, by applying the unconditional quantile regression (UQR) approach. This approach can address the traditional quantile regression approach's limitation that its distributions are defined conditional on specific covariates. Specifically, we not only examine the dependence structures among these six regional stock markets, but also explore the effect of global economic factors on them, given the strengthening of both international investment and the globalization of financial markets. The results show a heterogeneous dependence structure for the different quantiles of regional stock markets. Moreover, this dependence structure is often an asymmetric u-shaped or n-shaped structure, which indicates that the impacts of both other regional stock markets and economic factors are more pronounced during bear and bull markets than during normal markets, especially so in bear markets.

This thesis explains how global external factors affect stock markets according to different periods and market conditions, and proves usefulness of considering global external factors in the models. These findings will assist policymakers (investors) in designing better policies (portfolios) and assist researchers in building more accurate models.

Contents

List of Tables

List of Figures

Chapter 1

Introduction

1.1 Background and Motivation of the Research

"It has been said that something as small as the flutter of a butterfly's wing can ultimately cause a typhoon halfway around the world."

<The Butterfly Effect>

In recent years, the globalization and integration of financial markets bring many opportunities to domestic markets and international investors. However, this trend has also increased stock markets exposure to shocks of global external factors, which leads to more sensitive and fragile stock markets. Despite internal factors that can occur within own market will affect stock prices, today's stock markets are more affected by a series of global external factors than they were 20 years ago. Thus, the present thesis contains three studies on the global stock market nexus considering external factors. In this thesis, we divide global external factors into two major categories, namely, other regions or types of stock markets and global economic factors. Specifically, we not only examine the relationships among stock markets, but also explore the impact of global economic factors on them.

According to the butterfly effect, coined by Edward Lorenz (Lorenz, 1963), two things that do not seem to be connected actually affect each other, a very small change in one of the external factors can create a significantly different outcome. Kelsey (1988) indicates that economics and weather forecasting have a lot in common; both are trying to predict the outcomes of very large systems, the components of which mutually interact in complex ways. A large number of contingent global external factors that potentially change over time can affect stock prices, therefore, the current stock markets are full of randomness and contingency.

The chaos theory had been observed in a wide variety of natural sciences for decades and it caught the attention of the economic and financial fields from the 80s of the last century (Day, 1983, 1992; Brock and Hommes, 1998; Shintani and Linton, 2004). The chaotic behaviour has the main properties: randomness, nonlinearity, multicomponentness, and openness of a system. Due to the globalization and increasing randomness in financial markets, stock markets are also increasingly in line with these properties. Hence, we should think of stock markets as a complex system that is influenced by numerous external factors, and consider the global financial market as a whole to analyse, which allows our study to be brought closer to reality. In the three-body problem, if there are more than three individuals interacting with each other, their influence path is complex and unpredictable. Similar to natural science, numerous global external factors also affect stock markets in nonlinear ways, which requires that we should apply nonlinear models to study realistic economic issues.

We show some practical examples to explain how global external factors affect stock markets.

First, due to contagion effects between stock markets, stock markets will be affected by their counterpart of other regions or countries. Usually, contagion effects between stock markets with similar market structure is more pronounced, because they often face the same economic situation. However, we cannot ignore the spillover effects of developed stock markets because of their dominant position in the world economy. A very typical example, during the 2007—2009 global financial crisis, the collapse of the U. S. stock market led to a decline in global stock markets. In addition, The contagion effects between stock markets are not static, they become stronger during periods of market turbulence.

Second, changes in monetary policy of developed markets will affect stock markets, especially U. S. market. For example, rising U. S. interest rate and U. S. dollar appreciation will increase the pressure of capital outflow in other countries, and investors will change their domestic currency into U. S. currency, thereby reducing the domestic money supply and stock prices in other countries. Despite Federal Reserve is well aware of this fact and does consider global concerns into its monetary policy decisions, which does not mean that its policy will not have an impact on stock markets. Moreover, uncertainty in U. S. economic and monetary policy will bring greater volatility to global stock markets.

Third, Black Swan events have occurred more frequently in recent years, which can cause massive consequences for stock markets, thereby increasing the volatility of stock markets. It is like the "9 · 11 attacks", the Euro debt crisis, and the Brexit event, Black Swan events are typically unexpected. They seem to have no connection with stock markets, but actually affect stock markets, which is consistent with the butterfly effect. Even though this type of events can be positive or negative, they often lead to huge crashes in global stock markets; thus, we should pay more attention to how global external factors affect stock markets under different market conditions, especially in bear market.

Next, we have three questions about how global external factors affect stock markets. First, are the speed and intensity of transmission mechanism of different global external factors consistent (Chapter 2). In fact, the sensitivity of stock markets to each external variable is different. The transmission mechanism of financial variables (e.g. developed stock and exchange rate markets) may be faster than that of other variables in the short term. However, their influence will disappear quickly, because stock markets have random walk characteristics, and international capital flows are relatively rapid. On the contrary, there are some other variables that have a slower impact on stock markets. Moreover, the information transmission intensity of global external factors can change over time. For example, during the 2007—2009 global financial crisis, the number of variables affecting stock markets will increase significantly. This requires that we should analyse the impact of global external factors on stock markets in a dynamic perspective.

Second, can we prove that we will obtain more accurate and better results when considering global external factors in the model (Chapter 3). The globalization of financial markets has increased stock markets exposure to exogenous shocks, and the shocks in developed markets often increase risk in global stock markets. Hence, we will incorporate exogenous shocks into our model, and then evaluate the usefulness of incorporating these exogenous shocks. This approach not only can identify the spillover channels of external risk, maybe it can also improve the accuracy of our model and provide better information for investors, because it brings our model closer to the real world.

Third, will the structure and degree of influence of global external factors on stock markets change according to different market conditions (Chapter 4). According to the efficient market hypothesis (Fama,

1970, 1998), stock prices reflect all available information and investors are expected to act rationally. However, there are many extreme market conditions in real stock markets, and Black Swan events often bring bear market. Investors' fear (greed) is magnified in bear (bull) markets because of their herding behaviour. Thus, stock markets will overreact to changes in other stock markets and global economic factors under extreme market conditions. Given this situation, we systematically explore the dependence structures for regional stock markets, considering different market conditions, mainly in bear or bull markets compared with normal markets.

Overall, today's stock markets have become more complicated and unpredictable due to globalization and marketization of financial markets, we need to carefully consider how global external factors affect stock markets under different times and market conditions. Moreover, there are a large number of global external factors that can influence stock markets. Since these global external factors have different economic properties, they will play their respective roles that have a positive or negative effect on stock markets. Hence, we argue that selecting numerous global external factors for the analysis yields more comprehensive information for researchers and investors.

1.2 Selection of Global External Factors

As mentioned before, the internal factors that occur within own market will also affect stock prices. For example, changes in domestic business cycle, economic policy, and money supply will significantly affect domestic stock prices. In addition, Fama and French (1992, 2015) present famous the three-factor model and the five-factor model that is more concerned with internal factors of listed companies.

However, we only focus on global external factors in this thesis, because these factors are common factor and we want to know which global external factors are major and which global external factors are minor in exploring stock prices, while incorporating internal factors make these difficult to identify. Moreover, empirical studies in recent years present that the global external factors are more predominant over country internal factors in explaining stock prices during periods of financial globalization (Kenourgios and Dimitriou, 2015; Prabheesh and Vidya, 2018).

To study how global external factors affect stock markets from a more detailed perspective, we think that it is necessary to divide global external factors into two major categories, namely, other stock markets and global economic factors. On the one hand, exploring how stock markets interact with each other is one of the important works of this thesis, given that contagion effects between stock markets have become stronger in recent years. Thus, we select numerous stock markets from different market characteristics and regional perspectives, such as emerging and developed stock markets, and global six regional stock markets. According to the Markowitz (1952) portfolio theory, creating a diversified portfolio of multiple assets that are less relevant can reduce risk, which drives investors to diversify their assets across borders and regions, highlighting the importance of investigating the relationships among stock markets (Nasser and Hajilee, 2016; Mensi et al., 2017).

On the other hand, exploring how global economic factors affect stock markets is also one of the important works of this thesis. Since global economic factors have their own economic significance and their channels of influence on stock markets are different, these global economic factors are subdivided into two groups of variables. Specifically, the first group of variables represents the market situations and the second group of variables has a direct causal relationship with stock markets.

As for the variables that represent the market situations, they can indirectly affect stock markets. For example, a rising business cycle will bring an increase in economic output and profits, thereby influencing stock prices. Moreover, when economic fundamentals worsen or financial markets are full of pressure and uncertainty, fearful investors will sell assets perceived as risky and instead purchase safer assets according to the "flight-to-quality" effect. This behaviour can worsen financial market conditions and deteriorating financial market conditions will further exacerbate stock price declines. Thus, we consider the following variables to represent the market situations.

- Global business cycle

Generally speaking, stock markets reflect real economic activity, because higher economic growth can help companies be more profitable. Entorf et al. (2012) indicates that positive (negative) news regarding business cycle can bring an increase (decrease) of stock prices. The role of global business cycle is growing due to financial market globalization, this thesis selects OECD industrial production to represent global business cycle.

- Risk and liquidity of financial markets

Many literature find significant volatility spillovers from the U. S. stock market to the other stock markets (Balli et al., 2015). Moreover, liquidity of financial markets is an important variable, because it refers to how much investor interest and attention the current stock markets. To measure the risk and liquidity of global financial markets, we apply Chudik and Fratzscher's (2011) approach that uses two financial stress indices, namely, the implied volatility of the S&P 500 index (VIX) and the TED spread.

- U. S. economic and monetary policy uncertainty

Uncertain U. S. economic and monetary policies will make global market full of unknowns, which increase the cost for forecasting stock prices, thereby influencing investor sentiment and market stability. This thesis selects not only Baker et al. 's (2012) the U. S. economic policy uncertainty index (EPU), but also Husted et al. 's (2017) the U. S. monetary policy uncertainty index (MPU), because the definitions of these two indices are different.

Regarding the variables that have causal relationships with stock markets, they can directly affect stock markets. In other words, changes in these variables can directly lead to rises and falls of stock prices. For instance, a large amount of global capital inflows and high investor sentiment can quickly bring about an increase in stock prices. Moreover, the price of oil as a global commodity representative could directly affect stock prices, especially in extreme market conditions. Thus, we consider the following variables to analyse how they affect stock markets.

- U. S. monetary policy

Adjusting interest rate is the most commonly used monetary policy, changes in U. S. monetary policy will affect both its own stock market and other stock markets because of its leading position in the global economy. Moreover, Laopodis (2013) presents that different monetary regimes have asymmetric effect on stock markets. We select the U. S.

federal funds rate to represent the U. S. interest rate, which can help us understand how U. S. monetary policy influences stock markets.

- Global capital flows

Despite changes in both the U. S. interest rate and foreign currency value can lead to considerable international capital flows, change in foreign exchange rates may have a more direct and rapid impact on stock prices. Hence, we use the trade-weighted USD index to evaluate the value of U. S. dollar that is the world's most important currency. According to the "stock-oriented" model of exchange rates (Branson, 1983), there is a negative relationship between the stock and foreign exchange markets.

- Global commodity markets

Owing to financialization of commodity markets, we consider global all commodity markets and two influential commodity markets, namely West Texas Intermediate (WTI) crude oil and gold. Generally, oil prices are a synchronous macroeconomic indicator of early economic expansion (Chen and Lv, 2015), and gold has a safe haven property against stock markets during periods of market turbulence (Baur and Lucey, 2010).

- Global investor sentiment

With the increasing importance of behavioural finance theory, investor sentiment (Baker and Wurgler, 2006; Shiller, 2015) has become a critical variable when exploring stock prices. Moreover, investor sentiment overreacts to changes in stock markets under extreme market conditions. We select the OECD consumer confidence index to represent global investor sentiment, which is an additional factor beyond the traditional variables. In addition, the VIX and TED spread can also be indirectly considered to represent investor sentiment.

1.3 Objects and Methods of the Research

In the past few decades, the emerging Asian markets have been making remarkable headway in the process of economic and financial reform. Today, the emerging Asian markets are one of the fastest growing economies in the world, researchers and international investors have shown considerable interest in the these stock markets (Chien et al., 2015; Li and Giles, 2015). Thus, Chapter 2 and Chapter 3 are focused on the emerging Asian stock markets.

Moreover, due to the growing number of regional economic agreements (e.g. EU, NAFTA, ASEAN, MERCOSUR, Gulf Cooperation Council) and the current trend towards regional financial integration, such a regional insight can provide important information for global policymakers and investors (Guesmi and Nguyen, 2011; Kenourgios and Padhi, 2012). Hence, Chapter 4 focuses on global regional stock markets instead of individual stock markets.

More sensitive global financial markets lead to complex and irregular behaviour in stock markets, and these behaviours are consistent with some properties of the chaos theory. The chaos theory is characterized by strong nonlinearity, and chaotic economics can also be called nonlinear economics. Since the 1980s, many economists found evidence for nonlinear structures in macroeconomic (Beaudry and Koop, 1993) and financial (Bollerslev et al., 1992) time series. Similarly, the influence of numerous global external factors on stock markets is also nonlinear.

Moreover, to better answer the three questions raised earlier, we apply three different nonlinear models to analyse the impact of global external factors on stock markets.

Chapter 2 adopts the dynamic model averaging (DMA) approach to analyse the global economic factors that impact on emerging Asian stock market returns. One of the advantages of the DMA approach is that both forecasting models and their coefficients can change over time, which is important for a financial asset that is influenced by a variety of potential time-varying factors (Koop and Korobilis, 2012). Moreover, unlike existing DMA studies that only considered forecasting asset prices, this study considers both the relationship for the current period and the prediction for the next month due to the sensitivity of stock markets.

Chapter 3 applies the ARMA-cDCC-FIEGARCH model to the emerging Asian and other global stock markets. More importantly, to explore the potential effect of exogenous shocks on volatility of stock markets, we add the implied volatility of the S&P 500 index (VIX) and the U. S. economic policy uncertainty index (EPU) to the ARMA-cDCC-FIEGARCH model. Moreover, we also evaluate the usefulness of incorporating exogenous shocks in our models through the value at risk (VaR) analysis and two hedging effectiveness measures.

Chapter 4 uses Firpo et al.'s (2009) unconditional quantile regression (UQR) approach to capture the dependence structures for six regional stock markets, as this approach can provide the detailed dependence structures for different stock market conditions. Moreover, the UQR approach could provide more accurate extreme-value relationships than traditional quantile regression approach. Specifically, this study examines both the dependence structures among and the effect of global economic factors on six regional stock markets.

To summarise, this thesis does a good job as an empirical finance research. Because it provides novel and detailed empirical evidences on how global external factors affect stock markets according to different periods and market conditions, and proves usefulness of considering external factors shocks in the models, which can assist policymakers (investors) in creating better policies (portfolios) and assist researchers in building more accurate models.

Chapter 2

What Global Economic Factors Drive Emerging Asian Stock Market Returns? Evidence from a Dynamic Model Averaging Approach

2.1 Introduction

In the past few decades, marketization and the continuous opening-up of emerging Asian markets has led to their increasing relevance to the world economy, as became evident during the 1997—1998 Asian financial crisis. In other words, the emerging Asian markets are increasingly affected by global economic factors such as the global business cycle, developed stock markets, international capital flows, and global investor sentiment.

The influence of global factors on stock markets has received considerable attention from academic researchers, portfolio risk managers, and policymakers. Mollah et al. (2016) examined MSCI daily indices from 55 stock markets and found that contagion spread from the United States (U. S.) to global stock markets during the global financial and eurozone crises. Nasser and Hajilee (2016) found evidence of the existence of short-run integration among stock markets in emerging countries and developed markets, using a cointegration and error correction model. Sugimoto et al. (2014) applied the spillover index approach and discovered that African stock markets are most severely affected by spillovers from global stock markets and only modestly by global commodity and currency markets. Moreover, many existing studies have focused on the influence of global factors on the Gulf Cooperation Countries (GCC) stock markets (Jouini, 2013; Balcilar et al., 2014; Aloui et al., 2015; Mensi et al., 2017) and BRICS (Brazil,

Russia, India, China, and South Africa) stock markets (Hwang et al., 2013; Hammoudeh et al., 2013; Mensi et al., 2014). In terms of the emerging Asian stock markets, Richards (2005) suggested that foreign investors and external conditions have a larger impact on emerging Asian markets. Using the asymmetric BEKK model, Li and Giles (2015) reported significant unidirectional shock and volatility spillovers from the U. S. market to the emerging Asian markets. Kim et al. (2015) found foreign investors had a substantial role in correlations across the U. S. and emerging Asian markets.

Despite existing studies having employed a variety of econometric models to examine the influence of global factors on stock markets, these approaches all have several disadvantages as follows:

First, the models used in existing studies do not allow both parameters and coefficients to change over time, which is not suitable for exploring stock prices that are influenced by a series of external economic factors which potentially change under different market conditions.

Second, the models used by existing studies only considered a few variables as global factors. If a large number of variables is selected, these models will face difficulties in calculations.

Third, most existing studies adopted general econometric models to examine the in-sample relationship between stock prices and global factors.

However, there is no established forecasting model for stock prices that simultaneously considers many potential factors.

To address the disadvantages mentioned above, this study applies the dynamic model averaging (DMA) approach developed by Raftery et al. (2010), which performs quite well in macroeconomic forecasting (Koop and Korobilis, 2011, 2012). This novel approach allows for the coefficients of variables to evolve over time and for the forecasting model to change over time. Moreover, if m (=10) potential variables need to be considered in the model, the DMA framework allows the researcher to have 2^m(=1024) models to choose from, which increases the flexibility to capture unexpected changes in stock prices. Due to these advantages of the DMA framework, this approach has been successfully applied to forecast inflation (Koop and Korobilis, 2011; Filippo, 2015), gold prices (Aye et al., 2015; Baur et al., 2016), oil prices (Drachal, 2016; Naser, 2016), housing prices (Bork and Moller, 2015; Risse and Kern, 2016; Wei and Cao, 2017), and China's foreign exchange reserves (Gupta et al., 2014).

To the best of our knowledge, while some studies have examined economic variables and asset prices mentioned above, few have explored the prices of stock markets using the DMA approach. Figure 2.1 shows the monthly returns behaviour for emerging Asian stock markets.[①] According to Figure 2.1, we find a strong variation of stock returns in emerging Asian markets, which indicates that the factors affecting stock prices also change over time and that the use of the DMA approach is appropriate. Against this background, this study adopts the DMA approach to analyse stock returns in emerging Asian markets, and we selected the global business cycle, economic and monetary policy uncertainty indices, financial and commodity markets, and investor sentiment as global economic factors. Although regional economic factors and contagion effects between Asian stock markets will also affect stock returns, we only considered global factors in this study. Because

① The monthly returns behaviour for all the emerging Asian stock markets is similar, here we only provide the examples of China and Korea.

global factors are common factor and we want to know which global factors are major and which global factors are minor in exploring stock returns, while incorporating other factors make these difficult to identify. Similarly, domestic factors are also not considered in this study. For example, different exchange rate regimes lead to different exchange rate dynamics, and thus, we used the trade-weighted U. S. dollars (USD) index instead of the exchange rate of each market. Moreover, Prabheesh and Vidya (2018) presented that the global business cycle is more predominant over country business cycles in explaining stock returns during periods of financial liberalization. It is also worth noting that we not only examined in-sample relationships, but also explored the out-of-sample predictability for the influence of global factors on stock returns in emerging Asian markets. Taking into account the random walk characteristics of emerging Asian stock markets (Füss, 2005), we think that it is appropriate to forecast for only one month and that long-term forecasting horizons result in over-prediction.

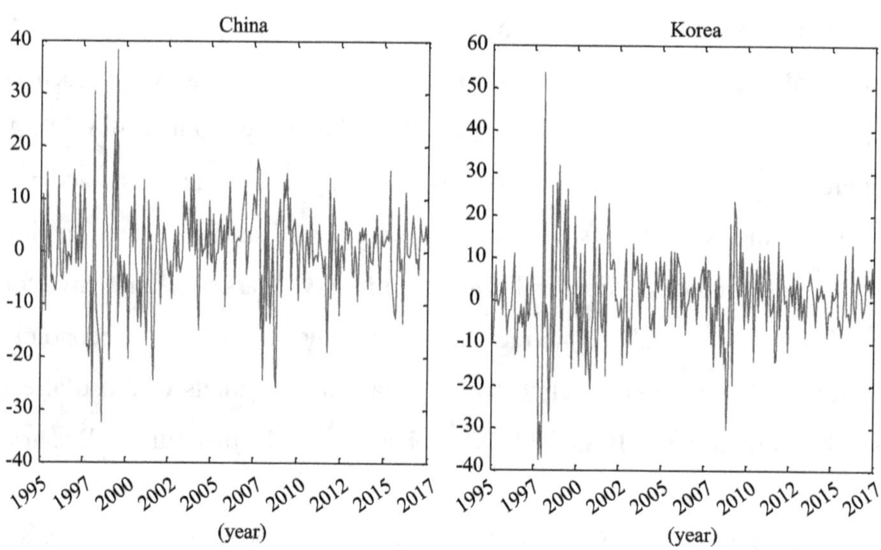

Figure 2.1 Monthly returns behaviour for emerging Asian stock markets (China and Korea)

This paper adds to and differs from existing studies in several aspects.

First, this paper is the first to use the DMA approach to analyse stock returns in emerging Asian markets. It is clear that the volatility of stock prices is larger than that of inflation, gold prices, and housing prices as reported by many existing studies using the DMA approach. Moreover, stock markets are financial markets that are influenced by a wide range of external economic factors. Thus, we believe that the DMA approach's advantage in allowing both the forecasting model and parameters to change with time is more suitable for capturing stock market behaviour.

Second, unlike existing studies that only considered forecasting economic variables or asset prices using the DMA approach, this paper considers both the relationship for the current period and the prediction for the next month, which is proposed in Baur et al. (2016). Due to their sensitivity, stock markets are more vulnerable to uncertainty in external factors compared to other financial markets; such external factors can immediately influence stock markets, highlighting the importance of exploring the in-sample relationship between stock returns and global factors.

Third, with the increasing importance of behavioural finance theory (BF), investor sentiment (Barberis et al., 1998; Baker and Wurgler, 2006; Shiller, 2015) has become a critical factor when investigating stock prices. This paper selects the OECD consumer confidence index to represent global investor sentiment, which can assist academic researchers and investors in understanding how the behaviour of market participants affects stock prices.

The structure of the rest of the paper is as follows: Section 2 provides the DMA framework. Section 3 describes our data, and Section 4 discusses the empirical results. Section 5 presents the conclusions.

2.2 Methodology

Despite the fact that traditional time-series models (multivariable regression or autoregression) can provide easy estimations, the disadvantage of their constant coefficients is also obvious. Time-varying parameter (TVP) models apply state space methods such as the Kalman filter, which allows the coefficients of explanatory variables to change over time. As noted by Primiceri (2005) and Cogley and Sargent (2005), the standard TVP model can be written as follows:

$$y_t = x_t\beta_t + \varepsilon_t \tag{2.1}$$

$$\beta_t = \beta_{t-1} + \eta_t \tag{2.2}$$

However, the TVP models have the potential drawback that they do not allow explanatory variables used in the forecasting model to change over time. Moreover, if the number of explanatory variables in x_t is large, these models tend to overfit in-sample and forecast poorly (Koop and Korobilis, 2012). Extensions of TVP models such as the TVP-VARs also suffer from the same problems (Koop and Korobilis, 2012). Fortunately, Raftery et al. (2010) present a novel method known as dynamic model averaging (DMA), which is frequently used in empirical macroeconomic research. The DMA approach allows both the forecasting models and their coefficients to change with time. The DMA model consists of the two following equations:

$$y_t = x_t^{(k)}\beta_t^{(k)} + \varepsilon_t^{(k)} \quad (2.3)$$

$$\beta_{t+1}^{(k)} = \beta_t^{(k)} + \eta_t^{(k)} \quad (2.4)$$

where y_t is the emerging Asian stock return (i. e. the log first difference of the stock spot price), $x_t^{(k)}$ denotes a vector of explanatory variables, and $\beta_t^{(k)}$ denotes a vector of coefficients. The innovation item $\varepsilon_t^{(k)}$ is $N(0, H_t^{(k)})$ and $\eta_t^{(k)}$ is $N(0, Q_t^{(k)})$. The superscript $k = 1, \cdots, K$ denotes a specific predictor set; if there are m explanatory variables, there can be $K = 2^m$ different forecasting models. Hence, both the explanatory variable vector $x_t^{(k)}$ and the state vector $\beta_t^{(k)}$ are different for each model, which allows both the forecasting model and its parameters to change with time.

Let $L_t = k$ if the process is governed by the k_{th} model at time t. The evolution can be determined by a $K \times K$ transition probability matrix, P, with elements $P_{i,j} = Pr(L_t = i | L_{t-1} = j)$ for $i, j = 1, \cdots, K$. Unless m is very small, P will be an enormous matrix that will lead to imprecise inference and excessive computation time (Koop and Korobilis, 2012). To achieve feasible computation, we use the approximations proposed by Raftery et al. (2010) that involve two forgetting factors, α and λ.

The parameter prediction equations using the Kalman filter obtain β_t^k using all information up to time $t-1$:

$$\beta_t^{(k)} | y^{t-1} \sim N(\hat{\beta}_{t-1}^{(k)}, R_t^{(k)}) \quad (2.5)$$

$$R_t^{(k)} = \frac{1}{\lambda} \Sigma_{t-1|t-1}^{(k)} \quad (2.6)$$

where formulae $\hat{\beta}_{t-1}^{(k)}$ and $\Sigma_{t-1|t-1}^{(k)}$ depend on $H_t^{(k)}$ and $Q_t^{(k)}$, and $y^{t-1} = \{y_1, \cdots, y_{t-1}\}$. Moreover, λ denotes the forgetting factor with $0 < \lambda \leqslant 1$. The value of the forgetting factor determines how rapidly the forecasting model and parameters evolve. In other words, forgetting factors with a relatively slow rate (e. g. $\alpha = 0.99 = \lambda$) lead to stable models, while forgetting factors with a relatively fast rate (e. g. $\alpha = 0.90 = \lambda$) bring about unstable models.

The parameter updating equations are then defined as follows:

$$\hat{\beta}_{t|t}^{(k)} = \hat{\beta}_{t|t-1}^{(k)} + R_t^{(k)} x_t^{(k)'} (H_t^{(k)} + x_t^{(k)} R_t^{(k)} x_t^{(k)'})^{-1} (y_t - x_t^{(k)} \hat{\beta}_{t-1}^{(k)}) \quad (2.7)$$

$$\Sigma_{t|t}^{(k)} = R_t^{(k)} - R_t^{(k)} x_t^{(k)'} (H_t^{(k)} + x_t^{(k)} R_t^{(k)} x_t^{(k)'})^{-1} x_t^{(k)} R_t^{(k)} \quad (2.8)$$

To achieve feasible computation and to avoid applying the Markov chain Monte Carlo (MCMC) method, Equation (2. 6) at first introduces a forgetting factor, λ, that prevents the model from estimating $Q_t^{(k)}$. Moreover, we use an exponentially weighted moving average (EWMA) to account for estimating the innovations variance, $H_t^{(k)}$. ①

The model prediction equation using the Kalman filter is illustrated by:

$$\pi_{t|t-1,k} = \frac{\pi_{t-1|t-1,k}^{\alpha}}{\sum_{l=1}^{K} \pi_{t-1|t-1,l}^{\alpha}} \quad (2.9)$$

where α is the other forgetting factor with $0 < \alpha \leqslant 1$ and is interpreted in a similar manner to λ.

The model updating equation is defined as follows:

$$\pi_{t|t,k} = \frac{\pi_{t|t-1,k} P_k(y_t | y^{t-1})}{\sum_{l=1}^{K} \pi_{t|t-1,l} P_l(y_t | y^{t-1})} \quad (2.10)$$

where $P_l(y_t | y^{t-1})$ denotes the predictive density for model l evaluated at y_t given by $N(x_t^{(l)} \hat{\beta}_{t-1}^{(l)},\ H_t^{(l)} + x_t^{(l)} R_t^{(l)} x_t^{(l)'})$. Equations (2. 5)—(2. 10) constitute the entire parameter and model prediction equations and their updating equations using the Kalman filter.

Finally, we estimate the probability of model k by $\pi_{t|t-1,k} = Pr\ (L_t$

---

① Koop and Korobilis (2012) indicate that we could use a stochastic volatility or ARCH specification for estimating $H_t^{(k)}$. However, to do this would greatly add to the computational burden.

$= k \mid y^{t-1})$. The DMA obtains the predictive result at each point in time by taking the weighted average of all possible models according to these probabilities, $\pi_{t \mid t-1, k}$. The DMA framework is computed as:

$$\hat{y}_t^{DMA} = \sum_{k=1}^{K} \pi_{t \mid t-1, k} x_t^{(k)} \hat{\beta}_{t-1}^{(k)} \tag{2.11}$$

The dynamic model selection (DMS) then chooses the model with the highest model probability, $\pi_{t \mid t-1}^{*}$, at each time point. The DMS framework is:

$$\hat{y}_t^{DMS} = \sum_{k=1}^{K} \pi_{t \mid t-1}^{*} x_t^{(k)} \hat{\beta}_{t-1}^{(k)} \tag{2.12}$$

Based on this econometric framework, we will explore how the impact of potential global economic factors on stock returns in emerging Asian markets has changed over time.

2.3 Data

This study analysis is based on monthly data; each of the time series considered consisted of 270 observations. The Morgan Stanley Capital Index (MSCI) database was used to obtain data for emerging Asian stock markets from January, 1995 to June, 2017, and all stock indices are denominated in USD in order to avoid the effects of national currency fluctuations on the indices. In this study, the emerging Asian markets include China, Korea, Taiwan, Hong Kong, Singapore, India, Malaysia, and Thailand. [①]

---

① The MSCI classifies China, Korea, Taiwan, India, Malaysia, and Thailand as emerging markets and classifies Hong Kong and Singapore as developed markets, while the *Economist* lists the last two markets as emerging markets. Marr and Reynard (2010) define Hong Kong and Singapore as "emerged" emerging markets. To be more comprehensive, we regard all eight markets as emerging markets in this study.

Based on the existing literature, 10 potential global determinants were selected. These global economic factors include: (i) the global business cycle as represented by OECD industrial production (IP); (ii) the U. S. economic policy uncertainty index (EPU), as introduced by Baker et al. (2012);[①] (iii) the U. S. monetary policy uncertainty index (MPU), as introduced by Husted et al. (2017); (iv) the MSCI world index as a representative stock price index for developed economies; (v) the implied volatility of the S&P 500 index as represented by the VIX index; (vi) the all commodity price index; (vii) the gold price measured in USD per ounce; (viii) the U. S. federal funds rate; (ix) the trade-weighted USD index; and (x) the OECD consumer confidence index (CCI), which is based on households' plans for major purchases and their economic situation. Data used in this study was taken from the sources listed in Table 2. 1.

Table 2. 1 The data set

Series ID	Code	Description	Source
IP	4	OECD industrial production	OECD
EPU	1	U. S. economic policy uncertainty index	EPU(www. policyuncertainty. com)
MPU	1	U. S. monetary policy uncertainty index	EPU(www. policyuncertainty. com)
MSCI	4	MSCI World Index	MSCI
VIX	1	Implied volatility of the S&P 500 index	CBOE (www. cboe. com)
Commodity	4	All commodity price index	IMF
Gold	4	Gold price measured in USD per ounce	World Gold Council
Interest	4	U. S. federal funds rate	FRED
USD	4	Trade weighted USD index	FRED
CCI	1	OECD consumer confidence index	OECD

Note: Codes 1 and 4 indicate no transformation and the first difference of the natural logarithm of the variable, respectively.

① The starting time of the global EPU index (Davis, 2016) is January 1997, therefore its use would restrict our sample period. To support the use of the U. S. EPU index instead of the Global EPU index, we compute the correlation between these two variables and find a high correlation of 0. 71.

The EPU index is a news-based economic policy index constructed from newspaper archives; an increase in the EPU index foreshadows a decline in economic growth and employment in the following months (Baker et al., 2012). Husted et al. (2017) constructed a monthly index of the MPU by searching for keywords related to monetary policy uncertainty in the *New York Times*, *Wall Street Journal*, and *Washington Post*. Since the definitions of these two indices are different, this study selected not only the EPU index, but also the MPU index.

Moreover, this study selected OECD industrial production to represent global economic fundamentals, because changes in the global economic growth have a strong bearing on rises and falls of stock markets. With the globalization of financial markets, the emerging Asian stock markets have been frequently affected by developed economies' stock markets (return and risk) and global commodity markets (all commodity and gold markets) in recent years, making it increasingly important to consider these global factors. Richards (2005) indicated that foreign capital flows can both increase and decrease stock prices in emerging Asian markets. Considerable international capital flows among the global currency markets may affect performance of stock markets. Hence, the U. S. interest rate and exchange rate factors were considered. According to the behavioural finance theory (BF), the information structure and characteristics of market participants systematically influence individuals' investment decisions as well as market outcomes. It is worth mentioning that we selected the OECD consumer confidence index to represent global investor sentiment, which is an additional factor beyond the traditional variables.

Finally, due to stationarity considerations for each time series, the EPU, MPU, VIX, and CCI variables were not transformed in any way, while the log first difference is taken for the other variables; their stationarity is therefore by construction. Appendix Figure 2. 1 presents the set of untransformed and transformed global economic factors.

2.4 Empirical Results

The empirical results are divided into two subsections. First, we provide results for the expected sizes of the models and then present evidence of which variables are good predictors of stock returns. Second, we compare the forecast performance of the DMA with $\alpha = 0.99 = \lambda$ to the TVP, Bayesian model averaging (BMA), [①] and DMA with $\alpha = 0.95$ *or* $0.90 = \lambda$. Unlike other financial markets (e. g. gold and housing markets), global economic factors can rapidly affect stock markets. Since we are using monthly data, this study not only considers the relationship of the current period ($h = 0$), but also considers the prediction of the next month ($h = 1$). There is no practical economic significance in choosing long-term forecasting horizons, because stock markets have random walk characteristics.

2.4.1 Probability of Inclusion

Figure 2. 2 provides the time-varying average number of variables

---

① Raftery et al. (2010) indicate that if $\alpha = 1 = \lambda$, then the DMA is equivalent to the BMA (Hoeting et al., 1999) without any forgetting.

included in the model using DMA with $\alpha = 0.99 = \lambda$. Clearly, the number of variables gradually increases for h = 0 and h = 1 over the evaluation period, indicating that emerging Asian stock markets are increasingly influenced by global economic conditions due to the strengthening of economic globalization. Particularly, we find that during the 1997—1998 Asian financial crisis and the 2007—2009 global financial crisis, the number of variables increased significantly, while during the 2001 "dot-com bubble" and 2011 European debt crisis, the number of variables increased slightly. Moreover, there are few variables included in China① before 2005 for h = 0, implying that the Chinese stock market was much less affected by global factors compared with other stock markets in the beginning period. China adopted a managed floating exchange rate regime in July, 2005, which sped up the inflow of international capital in China, thereby improving the globalization of the Chinese stock market. Figure 2.2 does not tell us which variables are important and how variables change over time, which we subsequently discuss.

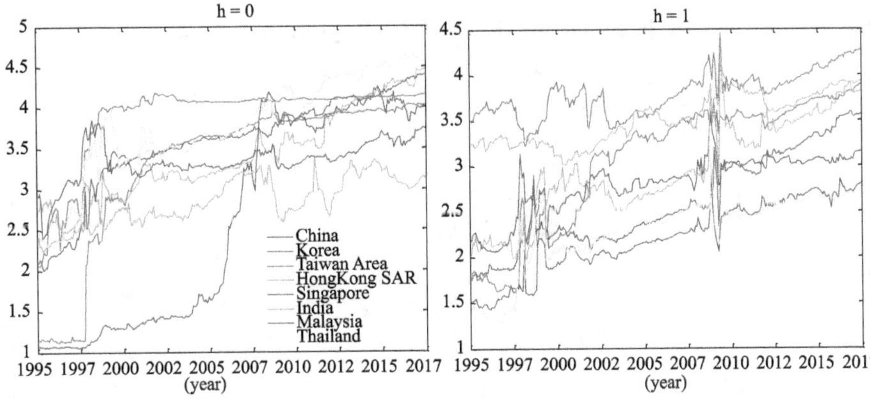

Figure 2.2 Expected sizes of the models over time for h = 0 and h = 1

① Throughout the article, China only refers to the Chinese mainland, excluding Taiwan area and Hongkong and Macao SARs.

Figure 2. 3 shows the inclusion probabilities of all variables for the current period ($h = 0$), using DMA with $\alpha = 0.99 = \lambda$. It is clear that all variables included in the model vary over time, providing important evidence to support the adoption of the DMA model. The study by Rapach et al. (2013) indicated that U. S. stock returns can provide predictive content for returns of numerous other countries. The integration of global financial markets shows evidence of the existence of contagion effects between emerging and developed stock markets (Sugimoto et al., 2014; Nasser and Hajilee, 2016), thus spillover effects from developed stock markets may significantly influence stock returns in emerging Asian markets. From Figure 2. 3, it can be seen that the developed stock markets (MSCI) have the strongest relationship with the emerging Asian stock markets, indicating that the information transmission mechanism between the stock markets is the fastest and strongest due to the globalization of financial markets. Interestingly, China and India's transmission mechanism from the developed stock markets is later than that of the other six markets, implying that the degree of globalization of these two markets is relatively low in the beginning period.

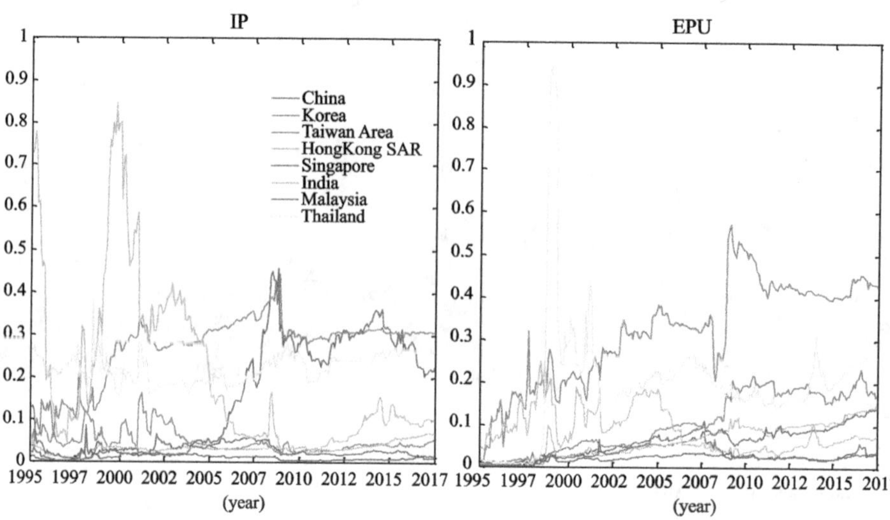

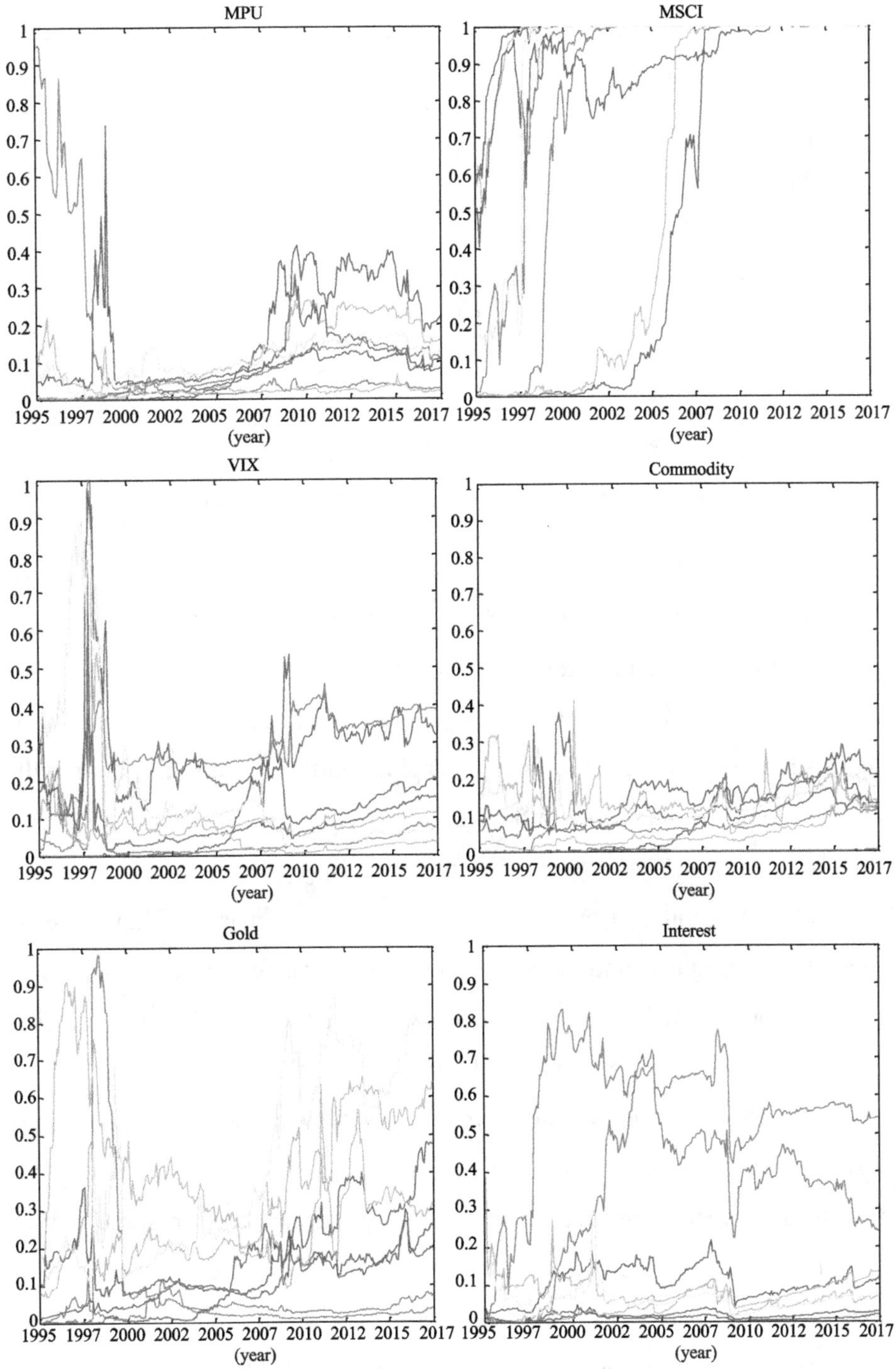
MPU
MSCI
VIX
Commodity
Gold
Interest
0 0.1 0.2 0.3 0.4 0.5 0.6 0.7 0.8 0.9 1
1995 1997 2000 2002 2005 2007 2010 2012 2015 2017
(year)

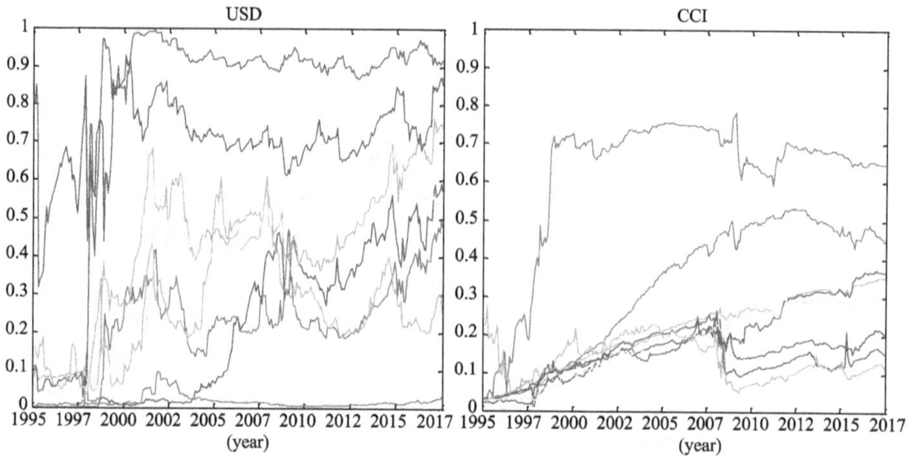

Figure 2. 3 Inclusion probabilities for various variables: h = 0

According to the " stock-oriented " model of exchange rates (Branson, 1983; Frankel, 1983), there is a negative relationship between the stock and foreign exchange markets (Liang et al., 2013; Reboredo et al., 2016). For example, domestic currency depreciation increases the pressure of domestic capital outflow, and investors will change domestic currency into foreign currency-denominated products, thereby reducing the domestic money supply and stock prices. International capital flows in global currency markets have been increasingly frequent and extensive during the past few decades, and we believe that capital inflows (outflows) increase (decrease) stock prices. Hence, in addition to developed stock markets, we find the U. S. exchange rate has the second strongest relationship with the emerging Asian stock markets, indicating that considerable international capital flows can affect performance in emerging Asian stock markets. We conclude that financial variables (developed stock markets and U. S. exchange rate) have a stronger relationship with emerging Asian stock markets than do other economic variables for h = 0, due to their stronger and more rapid information transmission capability. Moreover, the role of interest rates is obviously weaker than that of exchange rates, implying that the transmission mechanism of interest rates is slower. In other words, with the liberalization of emerging Asian exchange rate markets, changes in exchange rates can lead to more international capital flows in the short term compared with changes in interest rates.

Regarding the MPU index, we find that the transmission mechanism of monetary policy uncertainty is stronger for most stock markets following the 2007—2009 global financial crisis. This suggests that risk spillover effects from the U. S. monetary policy has become faster and stronger in recent years. For commodity markets, the role of the gold market is obviously stronger than that of other commodity markets, indicating that the transmission mechanism of gold is faster than that of the other commodity markets due to the safe haven property of gold. Concerning the CCI variable, ① we find that its role in emerging Asian stock markets gradually increases over time. Furthermore, we find that during the 1997—1998 Asian financial crisis and the 2007—2009 global financial crisis, the role of the study variables strengthened, especially in the IP, EPU, MPU, VIX, and gold variables. Increases in the EPU, MPU and VIX variables show risk spillover effects from the U. S. market got stronger, and the increase in the gold variable displays the safe haven role of gold becomes more important during extreme market periods.

Figure 2. 4 shows inclusion probabilities of all variables for the next

---

① Regarding the investor sentiment proxy, we also consider the other alternative sentiment indices such as the University of Michigan consumer sentiment index (CSI), AAII (American Association of Individual Investors) investor sentiment survey (ISS), and Investors Intelligence sentiment index (SI). We find that the CCI variable has more significant effect on stock returns by comparison with the CSI variable. Moreover, the ISS and SI variables are weekly data, while the sample frequency of our study is monthly. Thus, we finally select the CCI variable to represent global investor sentiment.

month ($h = 1$), using DMA with $\alpha = 0.99 = \lambda$. Interestingly, in contrast with the current period, the IP has the strongest predictive power among the 10 predictors considered. Generally speaking, the stock market reflects real economic activity, and Entorf et al. (2012) indicated that positive (negative) news regarding business cycle can bring an increase (decrease) of stock returns. For instance, an economic boom results in an increase in economic output, in which many companies experience increased profitability, thereby influencing stock prices. It is notable that the performance of global economic fundamentals with respect to market returns is not high for h = 0, whereas it is supreme predictive power among all predictors for h = 1; this indicates that there is a lag in the response of stock markets to the real economy. The predictive abilities (h = 1) of developed stock markets and exchange rates are currently lower than was the case previously (h = 0). Stock markets have random walk characteristics, and international capital flows are relatively rapid; thus, both of these financial variables influence stock returns in the short term. We conclude that the role of economic fundamentals is stronger than that of financial markets for the emerging Asian stock markets in the long term.

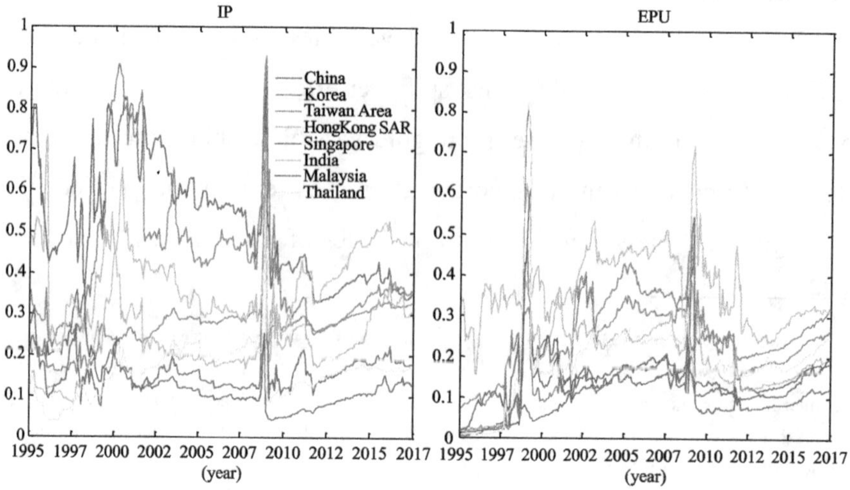

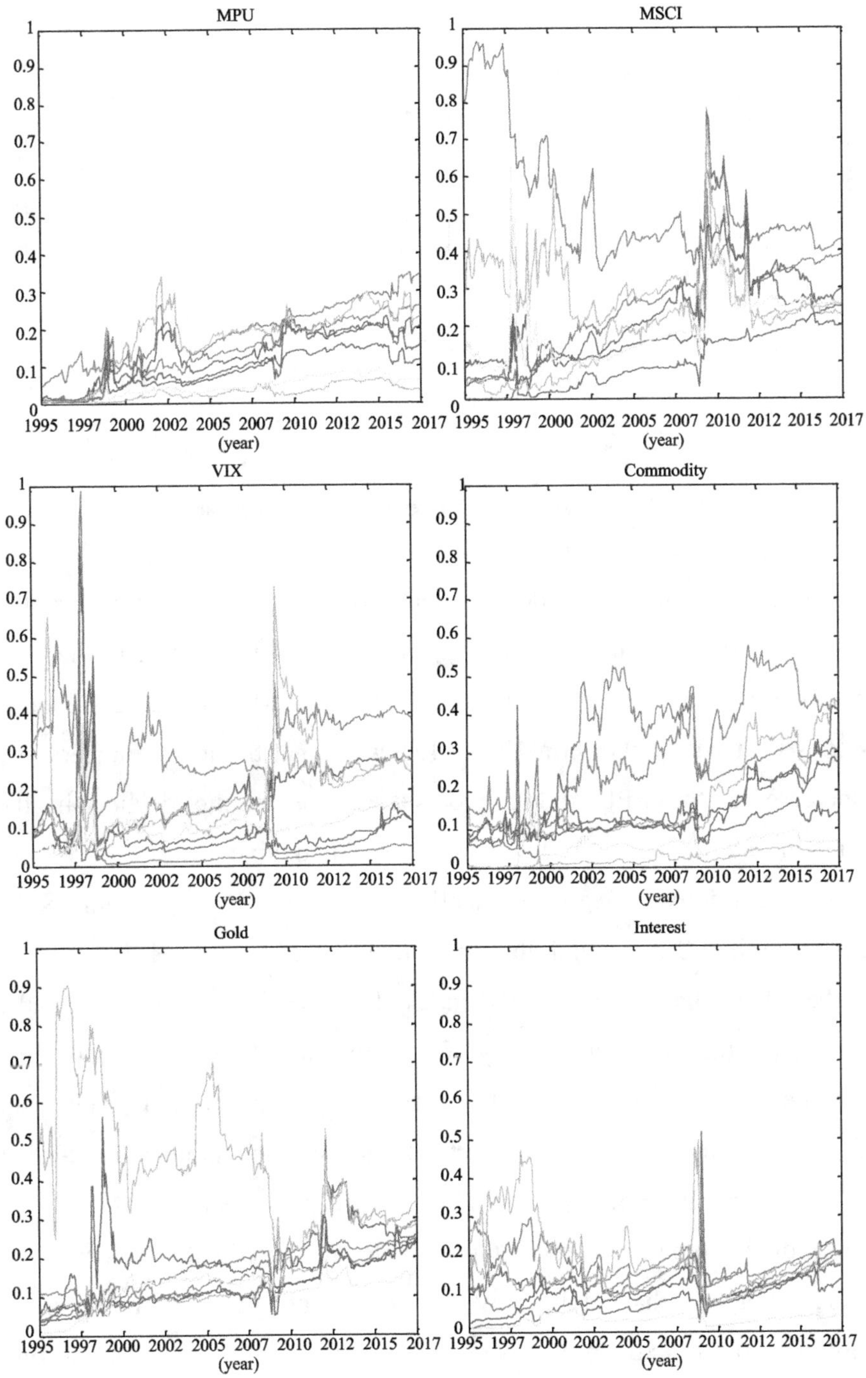
MPU
MSCI
VIX
Commodity
Gold
Interest
0 0.1 0.2 0.3 0.4 0.5 0.6 0.7 0.8 0.9 1
1995 1997 2000 2002 2005 2007 2010 2012 2015 2017
(year)

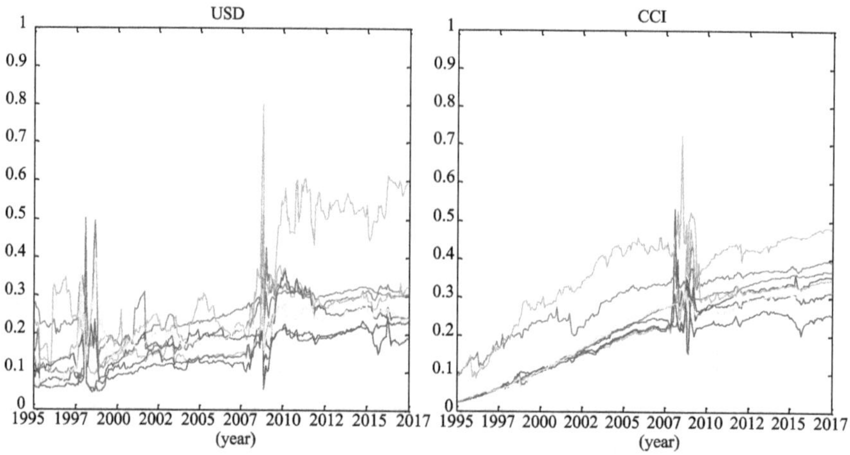

Figure 2. 4 Inclusion probabilities for various variables: h = 1

Moreover, the EPU index and all commodity markets show stronger predictive power for h = 1, indicating that the transmission mechanism of these two variables is relatively lagged. The lag effect of the EPU index is consistent with Baker et al. 's (2012) work that the market uncertainty (increase in the EPU index) foreshadows economic decline in the following months. For the MPU index, the predictive power of monetary policy uncertainty increases gradually over time. However, unlike the results for h = 0, we find the predictive power of the MPU index is weaker than that of the EPU index for h = 1, indicating that the information transmission intensity of the EPU and MPU indices is just the opposite for different periods. In other words, transmission mechanism of the U. S. monetary policy uncertainty is faster and shorter than that of the U. S. economic policy uncertainty. Similar to the results for h = 0, the predictive power of the CCI variable also gradually increases for h = 1, implying that global investor sentiment plays an increasingly important role in explaining stock prices, regardless of whether referring to in-sample or out-of-sample.

Regarding the influence of extreme turbulence, we observe the same pattern that inclusion probabilities of all variables significantly increase during the 1997—1998 Asian financial crisis and the 2007—2009 global financial crisis. More specifically, under the "flight-to-quality" effect, ① stock market liquidity declines when economic fundamentals worsen (Næs et al., 2011), which leads to a big fall in stock prices. Hence, role of IP becomes more important during these crises. Moreover, the predictive power of financial markets (developed stock markets, U. S. exchange rate and interest rate) also significantly increases during crises, because spillover effects between financial markets is stronger under extreme market conditions. Additionally, the increase in the EPU and VIX indices shows that volatility clustering of financial markets is more prominent during these crises, which provides evidence of the existence of structural breaks in financial markets. Finally, we compare the regional and global financial crises in terms of the global factors' impact on stock returns. Figures 2. 3 and 2. 4 show that transmission mechanisms of almost all global factors became more powerful during the 2007—2009 global financial crisis, except the VIX variable, indicating that in this recent crisis, a global factor's effect was more sound and faster than it was during the Asian financial crisis, given that globalization is more apparent nowadays than 20 years ago.

Overall, our results show strong support for the time variation of global factors that drive stock prices. Although inclusion probabilities of each variable exhibit differing patterns at different time points, the MSCI world index shows the strongest relationship with emerging Asian stock

---

① The "flight-to-quality" is the act of moving capital away from risky investments and toward safer investments (e. g. gold and U. S. Treasuries) under extreme market conditions.

markets for the current period ($h=0$), and the IP features the supreme forecasting power for emerging Asian stock markets for the next month ($h=1$). These important results suggest that investors should focus on developed stock markets to analyse current stock prices, and use global economic fundamentals to predict the next month's stock prices.

2.4.2 Model Performance

Selecting different forgetting factors (α and λ) can bring about different results. To compare the forecast performance for several alternative models, featuring either one or both forgetting factors fixed, we use not only the mean squared forecast error (MSFE), but also consider the sum of the log predictive likelihoods (log(PL)). Predictive likelihoods are Bayesian criteria, which do not only evaluate the point forecasts, but also consider the entire predictive distribution $P_l(y_t \mid y^{t-1})$ in model l; refer to Geweke and Amisano (2011) as a representative source.

In terms of the alternative models, we present results for:

(1) Models using DMA with $\alpha = 0.99 = \lambda$.

(2) Models using DMA with $\alpha = 0.95 = \lambda$.

(3) Models using DMA with $\alpha = 0.90 = \lambda$.

(4) Models using DMS with $\alpha = 0.99 = \lambda$.

(5) Models using DMS with $\alpha = 0.95 = \lambda$.

(6) Models using DMS with $\alpha = 0.90 = \lambda$.

(7) Models using a single model containing TVP in which all variables are included for all time periods, but coefficients are allowed to change (i. e. a special case of DMA where $\alpha = 1$ and $\lambda = 0.99$).

(8) Models using DMA, but where the coefficients do not vary over time (i.e. a special case of DMA where $\alpha = 0.99$ and $\lambda = 1$).

(9) Models using BMA (i.e. a special case of DMA where $\alpha = 1 = \lambda$).

Tables 2.2 and 2.3 provide the results for comparing different models for h = 0 and h = 1. According to the results, we find that the models do not perform equally well across all stock markets for h = 0 and h = 1. DMA with $\alpha = 0.99 = \lambda$ achieves relatively good performance for most markets when focusing on the MSFE, while the DMA with $\alpha = 0.90 = \lambda$ achieves relatively good performance for most markets when focusing on the log (PL). Hence, it is necessary to analyse results obtained from different forgetting factors.

Table 2.2 Comparing different models for stock price returns (1)

Model	h = 0		h = 1	
	MSFE	Log (PL)	MSFE	Log (PL)
		China		
DMA ($\alpha = 0.99 = \lambda$)	75.387	-955.107	98.774	-983.375
DMA ($\alpha = 0.95 = \lambda$)	79.774	-925.995	101.967	-973.130
DMA ($\alpha = 0.90 = \lambda$)	82.641	-924.842	101.354	-969.648
DMS ($\alpha = 0.99 = \lambda$)	81.747	-958.160	99.149	-988.959
DMS ($\alpha = 0.95 = \lambda$)	104.954	-932.741	118.328	-986.182
DMS ($\alpha = 0.90 = \lambda$)	104.901	-933.986	123.538	-987.222
TVP ($\alpha = 1$, $\lambda = 0.99$)	80.966	-962.692	93.959	-980.975
DMA ($\alpha = 0.99$, $\lambda = 1$)	75.923	-975.810	98.942	-990.959
BMA ($\alpha = 1 = \lambda$)	85.366	-984.143	94.207	-988.382

Continued

Model	h = 0		h = 1	
	MSFE	Log (PL)	MSFE	Log (PL)
		Korea		
DMA (α = 0.99 = λ)	79.416	-948.291	114.731	-1005.888
DMA (α = 0.95 = λ)	80.667	-906.646	120.978	-982.565
DMA (α = 0.90 = λ)	82.100	-902.976	120.205	-976.283
DMS (α = 0.99 = λ)	85.291	-958.822	128.519	-1021.645
DMS (α = 0.95 = λ)	91.468	-922.086	136.822	-994.654
DMS (α = 0.90 = λ)	90.294	-921.228	144.256	-991.033
TVP (α = 1, λ = 0.99)	82.398	-952.785	112.713	-1005.575
DMA (α = 0.99, λ = 1)	78.759	-969.915	115.593	-1017.515
BMA (α = 1 = λ)	80.629	-974.858	112.715	-1018.259
		Taiwan Area		
DMA (α = 0.99 = λ)	47.548	-889.607	64.873	-935.116
DMA (α = 0.95 = λ)	48.071	-871.387	67.064	-925.135
DMA (α = 0.90 = λ)	50.060	-874.918	67.013	-923.814
DMS (α = 0.99 = λ)	49.705	-890.141	70.991	-941.638
DMS (α = 0.95 = λ)	52.486	-874.892	74.300	-935.564
DMS (α = 0.90 = λ)	63.397	-888.177	76.488	-935.644
TVP (α = 1, λ = 0.99)	49.417	-890.404	64.666	-934.111
DMA (α = 0.99, λ = 1)	47.548	-908.826	64.690	-942.617
BMA (α = 1 = λ)	49.449	-909.230	64.646	-941.483
		Hong Kong SAR		
DMA (α = 0.99 = λ)	32.015	-823.814	54.023	-908.959
DMA (α = 0.95 = λ)	33.372	-813.082	53.779	-901.194
DMA (α = 0.90 = λ)	34.777	-815.211	52.738	-898.649
DMS (α = 0.99 = λ)	34.659	-829.929	60.266	-919.876
DMS (α = 0.95 = λ)	35.082	-820.570	65.122	-920.385
DMS (α = 0.90 = λ)	41.513	-838.253	64.090	-916.790
TVP (α = 1, λ = 0.99)	31.231	-823.483	51.766	-907.140
DMA (α = 0.99, λ = 1)	32.003	-837.244	53.677	-915.173
BMA (α = 1 = λ)	31.265	-836.926	51.438	-913.279

Table 2. 3 Comparing different models for stock price returns (2)

Model	h = 0		h = 1	
	MSFE	Log (PL)	MSFE	Log (PL)
		Singapore		
DMA ($\alpha = 0.99 = \lambda$)	24. 945	-808. 953	61. 882	-916. 995
DMA ($\alpha = 0.95 = \lambda$)	25. 248	-794. 083	60. 280	-904. 083
DMA ($\alpha = 0.90 = \lambda$)	26. 091	-794. 202	59. 645	-897. 841
DMS ($\alpha = 0.99 = \lambda$)	26. 073	-814. 016	63. 133	-928. 551
DMS ($\alpha = 0.95 = \lambda$)	27. 142	-801. 795	64. 503	-919. 597
DMS ($\alpha = 0.90 = \lambda$)	29. 014	-808. 617	70. 955	-916. 382
TVP ($\alpha = 1$, $\lambda = 0.99$)	25. 467	-810. 005	60. 255	-917. 143
DMA ($\alpha = 0.99$, $\lambda = 1$)	24. 972	-819. 191	61. 596	-920. 877
BMA ($\alpha = 1 = \lambda$)	25. 440	-819. 843	60. 136	-921. 091
		India		
DMA ($\alpha = 0.99 = \lambda$)	53. 576	-919. 672	82. 200	-960. 202
DMA ($\alpha = 0.95 = \lambda$)	54. 909	-915. 499	80. 836	-956. 986
DMA ($\alpha = 0.90 = \lambda$)	56. 074	-918. 792	82. 838	-960. 698
DMS ($\alpha = 0.99 = \lambda$)	59. 970	-926. 241	86. 891	-973. 530
DMS ($\alpha = 0.95 = \lambda$)	71. 921	-930. 138	99. 870	-977. 532
DMS ($\alpha = 0.90 = \lambda$)	73. 455	-939. 364	110. 880	-986. 882
TVP ($\alpha = 1$, $\lambda = 0.99$)	54. 916	-921. 620	81. 602	-962. 570
DMA ($\alpha = 0.99$, $\lambda = 1$)	53. 790	-927. 956	82. 666	-961. 528
BMA ($\alpha = 1 = \lambda$)	55. 245	-929. 777	81. 906	-963. 696
		Malaysia		
DMA ($\alpha = 0.99 = \lambda$)	50. 178	-892. 798	65. 384	-929. 003
DMA ($\alpha = 0.95 = \lambda$)	49. 643	-856. 132	67. 934	-901. 743
DMA ($\alpha = 0.90 = \lambda$)	48. 507	-848. 263	67. 608	-892. 412
DMS ($\alpha = 0.99 = \lambda$)	55. 711	-898. 738	68. 570	-931. 785
DMS ($\alpha = 0.95 = \lambda$)	66. 682	-870. 032	75. 784	-915. 273
DMS ($\alpha = 0.90 = \lambda$)	71. 973	-876. 015	80. 886	-913. 992
TVP ($\alpha = 1$, $\lambda = 0.99$)	50. 921	-890. 815	64. 446	-926. 696
DMA ($\alpha = 0.99$, $\lambda = 1$)	50. 246	-914. 413	65. 517	-947. 950
BMA ($\alpha = 1 = \lambda$)	51. 131	-913. 180	64. 645	-945. 244

Continued

Model	h = 0		h = 1	
	MSFE	Log (PL)	MSFE	Log (PL)
		Thailand		
DMA ($\alpha = 0.99 = \lambda$)	83. 303	-960. 197	121. 846	-1007. 994
DMA ($\alpha = 0.95 = \lambda$)	81. 876	-934. 336	131. 136	-986. 907
DMA ($\alpha = 0.90 = \lambda$)	84. 071	-935. 462	129. 453	-981. 987
DMS ($\alpha = 0.99 = \lambda$)	95. 007	-972. 247	137. 644	-1021. 393
DMS ($\alpha = 0.95 = \lambda$)	88. 253	-934. 554	163. 672	-1007. 649
DMS ($\alpha = 0.90 = \lambda$)	92. 419	-945. 134	165. 021	-995. 498
TVP ($\alpha = 1$, $\lambda = 0.99$)	84. 594	-961. 794	115. 156	-1006. 674
DMA ($\alpha = 0.99$, $\lambda = 1$)	83. 459	-977. 579	121. 964	-1021. 166
BMA ($\alpha = 1 = \lambda$)	85. 273	-978. 355	115. 873	-1020. 022

Drachal (2016) indicates that forgetting factors are responsible for how the previous estimations are remembered by the process for the current prediction in the time-varying coefficient framework, which can control the degree of instability in the coefficients. Following Koop and Korobilis (2012), forgetting factors with a relatively slow rate (e. g. $\alpha = 0.99 = \lambda$) lead to stable models where coefficient change is gradual, while forgetting factors with a relatively fast rate (e. g. $\alpha = 0.95 = \lambda$) bring about unstable models in which coefficient change is quite rapid. The strong variation in stock returns suggests that the factors influencing stock prices are uncertain and vary over time. It seems that selecting forgetting factors with a relatively fast rate (e. g. $\alpha = 0.95$ or $0.90 = \lambda$) may obtain better results when the variability of coefficients is large. In fact, we find that inclusion probabilities of most variables in each stock market display very high values for almost all periods when using DMA with $\alpha = 0.95$ or $0.90 = \lambda$. These results make it difficult to identify which global factors are major and which global factors are minor in explaining stock price returns. Moreover, it is difficult to capture the impact of global and regional financial crises on stock markets by observing these results. In addition, Baur et al. (2016) suggest that rapidly changing coefficients produce instantaneous jumps in the estimated parameters and the posterior predictive model probabilities, which increase estimation errors. Thus, results with more information will be obtained when we use DMA with $\alpha = 0.99 = \lambda$, which provides investors with important implications.

When examining the other three alternative models, with either one or both forgetting factors fixed to one, we find several good results for the MSFE and log(PL). However, these alternative models do not allow both the forecasting model and the coefficients to change together, and therefore, fail to explain the uncertainty of potential factors in stock markets at each point in time. More importantly, we observe that inclusion probabilities of most variables for each stock market are close to zero when considering the TVP and BMA models, which lose a lot of useful information and have very poor performances in explaining the stock prices.

2.5 Conclusions

This study used the DMA approach to analyse the influence of global economic factors on stock returns in emerging Asian markets. One of the advantages of this approach is that both coefficients and the entire forecasting model can change over time, which is important for a financial asset that is influenced by a variety of potential time-varying factors. In this study, we not only analyse the in-sample relationship ($h = 0$) between stock markets and global factors, but also explore the out-of-sample predictability ($h = 1$) for stock markets based on global factors.

Empirical results show that compared with other alternative models nested in DMA, DMA with $\alpha = 0.99 = \lambda$ has the best performance for all stock markets, as it provides more useful information for investors. Moreover, the factors considered can command different relationships and predictive powers at each point in time both in-sample and out-of-sample, which provides important evidence to support using DMA models that allow coefficients and models to change over time. Furthermore, we find that emerging Asian stock markets are increasingly influenced by the global economic factors due to financial market liberalization and globalization. More specifically, the MSCI world index and U. S. exchange rate show a stronger relationship with emerging Asian stock markets than do the other factors for the current period ($h = 0$), while the IP is the supreme forecasting power for emerging Asian stock markets for the next month ($h = 1$). In other words, the transmission mechanism of financial variables is faster for stock markets in-sample, while economic fundamentals have stronger predictive power for stock markets out-of-sample. Additionally, the role of global factors was significantly stronger during the 1997—1998 Asian financial crisis and the 2007—2009 global financial crisis, especially during the latter crisis. Finally, we find the role of CCI in the emerging Asian stock markets gradually increases over time both in-sample and out-of-sample.

Our findings have several important implications for policymakers, researchers, and investors. The information transmission mechanism, from developed stock markets to emerging stock markets, is relatively strong and rapid due to the globalization of financial markets. Investors can predict emerging stock market returns based on developed stock market conditions, which can assist them in reducing cost for forecasting stock returns. Moreover, our results show that exchange rate markets have a strong relationship with emerging stock markets. Since foreign capital inflows (outflows) can increase (decrease) stock prices, governments should create a more attractive domestic investment environment to encourage international capital inflows. Importantly, economic fundamentals are of supreme importance for forecasting stock returns, implying that the real economy is the primary determinant of stock markets in the long term. Thus, governments need to ensure robust development of the real economy to promote long-term stock market growth.

Investors should keep in mind that there are many global economic factors that can affect stock returns, where the impacts of these global factors vary over time. Since some asset classes (e. g. gold and USD) can show a negative relationship with stock returns in both the short and long term, investors should consider constructing diversified portfolios including such assets, and they should also frequently adjust their portfolio strategy according to varying market conditions. In addition, variables related to global market uncertainty (e. g. EPU, MPU, and VIX) are having more effect on stock returns since the 2007—2009 global financial crisis. Today, black swan events occur more frequently, such that emerging Asian stock markets need an effective market mechanism for hedging against the risks imposed by global markets. Finally, our findings prove that investor optimism and pessimism are having an increasingly significant effect on stock returns; this is in contrast to the efficient market hypothesis (Fama, 1970, 1998), according to which stock prices reflect all available information and investor sentiment does not significantly impact stock prices. However, investors are often irrational, and their decisions can affect market outcomes in the real world under conditions of information asymmetry; thus, researchers should pay greater attention to behavioural finance theory.

Chapter 3

Exogenous Shocks, Dynamic Correlations, and Portfolio Risk Management for the Emerging Asian and Other Global Developed and Emerging Stock Markets

3. 1 Introduction

According to the Markowitz (1952) portfolio theory, creating a diversified portfolio of multiple assets that are less relevant can reduce risk, which drives investors to diversify their assets across borders. During the past few decades, international investors have shown considerable interest in the emerging Asian markets due to their enormous potential and praiseworthy economic growth (Cheung and Mak, 1992; Masih and Masih, 1999). However, in recent times the emerging Asian markets have been making remarkable headway in the process of economic and financial reform, including the degree of government regulation, exchange rate system reform, and domestic financial market and institutional development, and so on, which has led to foreign direct investment (FDI), originating from this region, increasing significantly. Bano and Tabbada (2015) indicate that FDI outflows are closely associated with high domestic savings, large foreign reserves, export orientation, and relatively large FDI inflows in the East (China, Korea, Taiwan Area, and Hong Kong SAR), Southeast (Singapore, Malaysia, and Thailand), and South (India) emerging Asian markets. Especially, Chinese outward FDI has increased substantially in recent years (Zhang and Daly, 2011; Ramasamy et al., 2012; Kolstad and Wiig, 2012) and in 2016 China has been more open to FDI than most developed economies, second only to the United States (UNCTAD, 2017). A large amount of FDI outflows have resulted in many emerging Asian market investors transacting in the stocks of other countries or regions, directly or indirectly, through various investment funds.

On the other hand, analysing the characteristics of financial market returns, volatility, and dynamic relationships have a great impact on investment and risk management of market participants, as well as on policymakers. The empirical literature has documented that stock markets exhibit some major stylized features, such as leptokurtic effect, volatility clustering, leverage effect, and long memory (Aloui, 2011; Dimitriou et al., 2013). For cross-correlations in stock markets, a lower correlation means higher gain from a diversified portfolio. It provides important information in terms of asset pricing, portfolio selection, and diversification opportunities. More importantly, globalization of financial markets has increased stock market exposure to exogenous shocks. For example, Mollah et al. (2016) found out about the contagion spread from the U. S. to the global stock markets during the global financial and eurozone crises. Li and Giles (2015) reported the significant unidirectional shock and volatility spillovers from the U. S. to the emerging Asian markets. Shen (2018) confirms that shocks in the U. S. substantially increase risk in major Asian stock markets, which is in line with its dominant power across the global stock markets.

Motivated by the aboves, we attempt to explore the time-varying correlations between emerging Asian and other global developed and emerging stock markets and compare the hedging role of including other global developed and emerging stock assets in the portfolio. Moreover, we also evaluate the usefulness of incorporating exogenous shocks in our models through the value at risk (VaR) analysis and two hedging effectiveness measures, thereby understanding the potential effect of exogenous shocks on dynamic correlations and portfolio strategies.

From a methodological viewpoint, we use the consistent dynamic conditional correlation-fractionally integrated exponential generalized autoregressive conditional heteroskedasticity (cDCC-FIEGARCH) model under the Student-t distributions. This model is similar to DCC-fractionally integrated asymmetric power autoregressive conditional heteroskedasticity (FIAPARCH) model. These two models enable us to capture dynamic relationships, leverage effects, and long memory property in the volatility processes. For example, Kang et al. (2016) investigate the asymmetric and long memory volatility properties and dynamic conditional correlations between BRICS (Brazil, Russia, India, China, and South Africa) stock markets and commodity markets, using the trivariate DCC-FIAPARCH model. Mensi et al. (2017) examine dynamic linkages and portfolio diversification between the major developed and BRICS stock markets by applying both the DCC-FIEGARCH and dynamic equicorrelation (DECO)-FIEGARCH models. Moreover, since external events can bring about structural breaks in financial markets, ignoring structural breaks in the GARCH models may lead to an overestimate of the degree of volatility persistence (Aggarwal et al., 1999; Lamoureux and Lastrapes, 1990). Many studies (Hammoudeh and Li, 2008; Wang and Moore, 2009; Kang et al., 2009; among others) include structural breaks in volatility processes via Inclán and Tiao's (1994) iterated cumulative sum of squares (ICSS) algorithm. In this study, to capture exogenous shocks from the U. S. market to the other stock markets, we will incorporate implied volatility of the S&P 500 index (VIX) and the U. S. economic policy uncertainty index (EPU) in the volatility processes of our model, and then compare the role of considering exogenous shocks and controlling structural breaks in the model.

Our study adds to and differs from the existing literature using the ARMA-cDCC-FIEGARCH model, with and without exogenous shocks. First, it examines the dynamic relationships between the emerging Asian stock markets and developed markets, which are mature markets with more advanced market mechanism, and the other global emerging markets, which are markets with similar characteristics as emerging Asian markets. To this end, we apply two classified stock indices, such as the MSCI world index and the MSCI emerging markets ex-Asia index. Second, unlike existing studies that pay attention to the hedging role of incorporating emerging stock assets in developed market stock portfolio (Masih and Masih, 1999; Mensi et al., 2017), this study considers the importance of holding the developed and other emerging stock assets in emerging Asian market portfolio due to increasing foreign stock investment from Asian markets. For example, if developed markets are weakly correlated with their emerging Asian counterparts, emerging Asian market investors can reduce risk by including developed market assets in their portfolios. Third, we propose a novel approach that includes exogenous shocks in the model, which can identify the spillover channels of external risk. Fortunately, we find that considering exogenous shocks can play the same role of controlling structural breaks in the model as it solves the problem of the degree of volatility persistence being overestimated in the GARCH model, thereby improving the accuracy of the ARMA-cDCC-FIEGARCH model. Finally, the results of Mensi et al. (2015a) fail to provide evidence of controlling structural breaks in the model that can bring better portfolio strategies. Incorporating exogenous shocks in our model can assist us in obtaining better VaR performance results and hedging strategies.

The rest of this paper proceeds as follows. Section 2 provides the methodology. Section 3 describes our data and conducts some preliminary analysis. Section 4 discusses the empirical results. Section 5 draws the conclusions and policy implications.

3.2 Methodology

3.2.1 The ARMA-cDCC-FIEGARCH Model

We examine the ARMA-cDCC-FIEGARCH model to explore the dynamic correlations between emerging Asian and other global stock markets. We presume that daily returns are governed by the following autoregressive moving average (ARMA) process:

$$r_t = \mu + \sum_{i=1}^{m} \varphi_i r_{t-i} + \varepsilon_t + \sum_{j=1}^{n} \theta_j \varepsilon_{t-j}, \quad with\ \varepsilon_t = z_t \sqrt{h_t} \tag{3.1}$$

where the z_t is standardized residual and conditional variance, h_t, is positive with a probability of one. The ARMA (p, q) model is appropriate when the dynamics of daily returns are explained by their own lagged behaviour (the AR part) as well as past unobserved shocks (the MA part). Moreover, we choose the appropriate order of the ARMA model in the return-generating process.

To consider the asymmetry and long memory features in conditional variance, Bollerslev and Mikkelsen (1996) present the FIEGARCH model by combining the FIGARCH model of Baillie et al. (1996) with the EGARCH model of Nelson (1991). The FIEGARCH(p, d, q) model can be expressed as:

$$\ln(h_t) = \omega + \eta(L)^{-1}(1-L)^{-d}[1+\beta(L)][\lambda_1 z_{t-1} + \lambda_2(|z_{t-1}| - E|z_{t-1}|)] \quad (3.2)$$

where $\omega \in [0, \infty)$, $|\beta| < 1$, long memory parameter $d \in [0, 1]$, and L denotes the lag operator. The leverage effect is measured by the sign effect coefficient λ_1 and the magnitude effect coefficient λ_2. Specifically, $\lambda_1 < 0$ and $\lambda_2 > 0$ mean that negative shocks have a stronger impact on volatility than positive shocks; the reverse applies if $\lambda_1 > 0$ and $\lambda_2 > 0$. Note that if $d = 0$, the FIEGARCH will be reduced to the EGARCH model, and when $d = 1$, this model is reduced to the IEGARCH model. The FIEGARCH is superior to the other two models because it can provide greater flexibility in modelling the conditional variance (Bollerslev and Mikkelsen, 1999). More importantly, global stock markets will be affected by the shocks from the U. S. market. Thus, to explore the potential effect of exogenous shocks on volatility of stock markets, we first employ the VIX and the EPU indices as exogenous shocks, and then add the change rate of these indices to Equation (3.2). We believe that considering exogenous shocks in the FIEGARCH model can assist us in calculating more accurate estimates of the model parameters and measuring the spillover effects of exogenous shocks on the volatility of stock markets.

Because we attempt to explore the relationships between emerging Asian and other global stock markets, a multivariate FIEGARCH model needs to be set up. Thus, we expose the multivariate FIEGARCH model with the consistent DCC (cDCC) approach of Aielli (2013). To use the cDCC model, we briefly review the DCC model of Engle (2002). In the DCC model, we decompose the variance-covariance matrix of residuals into:

$$H_t = D_t R_t D_t, \text{ with } D_t = diag(\sqrt{h_{ii,t}}) \quad (3.3)$$

In Equation (3.3), R_t is the matrix of time-varying conditional correlations and D_t is the diagonal matrix of conditional standard deviations for each of the return series, which we obtain by estimating a univariate ARMA-FIEGARCH model. Next, we define the structure of the DCC model as follows:

$$Q_t = (1 - \alpha_{DCC} - \beta_{DCC})\overline{Q} + \alpha_{DCC} z_{t-1} z'_{t-1} + \beta_{DCC} Q_{t-1}$$
$$\rho_t^{DCC} = R_t = [diag(Q_t)]^{-1/2} Q_t [diag(Q_t)]^{-1/2} \quad (3.4)$$

where Q_t is the covariance matrix of standardized residuals z_t and $\overline{Q} = E[z_t \quad z'_t]$ is the unconditional covariance matrix. The scalar parameters α_{DCC} and β_{DCC} must be non-negative and satisfy $(\alpha_{DCC} + \beta_{DCC}) < 1$ to ensure the positivity of the matrix Q_t.

In this context, Aielli (2013) indicates that the estimation of covariance matrix Q_t in the DCC model is inconsistent since $E[R_t] \neq E[Q_t]$, and suggests cDCC model with the following correlation-driving process:

$$Q_t = (1 - \alpha_{cDCC} - \beta_{cDCC})\overline{Q}^* + \alpha_{cDCC} \{[diag(Q_{t-1})]^{1/2} z_{t-1} z'_{t-1} [diag(Q_{t-1})]^{1/2}\} + \beta_{cDCC} Q_{t-1} \quad (3.5)$$

where $\overline{Q}^*$ is the unconditional covariance matrix of $(diag(Q_t))^{1/2} z_t$. Following Engle (2002), we conduct the estimation using a two-step, quasi-maximum likelihood (QML) estimation method. The likelihood function can be written as:

$$\log(L) = -\frac{1}{2}\Sigma_{t=1}^{T}[n\log(2\pi) + 2\log D_t + \log R_t + z'_t R_t^{-1} z_t] \quad (3.6)$$

3.2.2 Value at Risk (VaR) Forecasting

The VaR is a quantitative tool used to measure risk of portfolio during a defined period for a given probability (Kuester, 2006; Wu and Shieh, 2007). We examine the ARMA-cDCC-FIEGARCH model with and without exogenous shocks and use the empirical results to compute a one-day-ahead VaR under three innovation distribution assumptions for normal, Student-t, and skewed Student-t distributions. If the VaR performance results obtained from the model with exogenous shocks is better than the results from its counterpart, considering exogenous shocks in the model can improve the accuracy of calculations.

For instance, the normal distribution, the VaRs for long and short trading positions are given by:

$$VaR_{t,\,long} = \mu_t + q_\alpha \hat{\sigma}_t \tag{3.7}$$

$$VaR_{t,\,short} = \mu_t + q_{1-\alpha} \hat{\sigma}_t \tag{3.8}$$

where μ_t and $\hat{\sigma}_t$ are respectively the conditional mean (ARMA process) and standard deviation, and q_α is the left quantile of the normal distribution at $\alpha\%$, while $q_{1-\alpha}$ is the right quantile at $\alpha\%$. In this way, we also obtain the VaRs under the Student-t and skewed Student-t distributions.

Moreover, we assess the accuracy of VaR performance results through the Kupiec (1995) LR test, which examines the failure rate for the left and right tails of the return distribution. The Kupiec LR test is expressed as:

$$LRT = -2\ln[(1-\alpha)^{T-x}\alpha^{x}] + 2\ln[(1-\hat{f})^{T-x}\hat{f}^{x}] \tag{3.9}$$

where $\hat{f} = x/T$ and $\hat{f}$ is the estimated failure rate.

3.2.3 Optimal Portfolio Weight and Hedge Ratio

To more efficiently manage the emerging Asian and other global stock assets, we compute the optimal portfolio weight and the hedge ratio for building optimal hedging strategies based on the results of the ARMA-cDCC-FIEGARCH model, with and without exogenous shocks.

We consider a risk-minimizing portfolio comprised of emerging Asian and other global stock assets without reducing expected return. Following Kroner and Ng (1998), the portfolio weight of other global stock assets is given by:

$$w_t^G = \frac{h_t^A - h_t^{A,G}}{h_t^A - 2h_t^{A,G} + h_t^G} \tag{3.10}$$

$$w_t^{*G} = \begin{cases} 0, & \text{if } w_t^G < 0 \\ w_t^G, & \text{if } 0 \leqslant w_t^G \leqslant 1 \\ 1, & \text{if } w_t^G > 1 \end{cases} \tag{3.11}$$

where h_t^A and h_t^G refer respectively to the conditional variance of the emerging Asian and other global stock markets, and $h_t^{A,G}$ refers to the conditional covariance between the emerging Asian and other global stock markets at time t. The optimal portfolio weight of the emerging Asian stock asset is $(1 - w_t^{*G})$.

To minimize the risk of a one-dollar portfolio that is long in the other global stock assets, the investor should short β dollars of the emerging Asian stock asset. According to Kroner and Sultan (1993), the risk-minimizing hedge ratio is specified as follows:

$$\beta_t^A = \frac{h_t^{A,G}}{h_t^A} \tag{3.12}$$

3.3 Data and Preliminary Analysis

3.3.1 Data

In this study, we consider daily closing spot price index series for the eight emerging Asian stock markets: namely China, Korea, Taiwan Area, Hong Kong SAR, Singapore, India, Malaysia, and Thailand, as well as for the global developed and other emerging stock markets. The data are extracted from the Morgan Stanley Capital Index (MSCI) database and all stock indices are denominated in U. S. dollars (USD) in order to avoid the effects of national currency fluctuations on the indices, as indicated by Bekaert and Harvey (1995) and Dimitriou et al. (2013). This paper selects the MSCI world index to represent global developed stock markets, which captures large and mid-cap representation across 23 developed markets (DM). ① Despite the MSCI classifying Hong Kong SAR and Singapore as developed markets, the *Economist* lists these two markets as emerging markets and Marr and Reynard (2010) define Hong Kong SAR and Singapore as "emerged" emerging markets. The proportion of Hong Kong SAR and Singapore markets is very low in the MSCI world index. For a more comprehensive study of emerging Asian markets, we regard these two markets as emerging markets in this study.

① The MSCI world index includes: Australia, Austria, Belgium, Canada, Denmark, Finland, France, Germany, Hong Kong SAR, Ireland, Israel, Italy, Japan, Netherlands, New Zealand, Norway, Portugal, Singapore, Spain, Sweden, Switzerland, United Kingdom, and United States.

Moreover, this paper selects the MSCI emerging markets ex Asia index to represent other global emerging stock markets, which captures large and mid-cap representation across 15 Emerging Markets (EM), excluding Asia.[①] Thus, we consider almost all global developed and emerging stock markets in this paper.

Regarding two exogenous shock variables, the VIX[②] measures the stock market's expectation of volatility implied by S&P 500 index options, which represents the uncertainty of the U. S. stock market. The daily news-based EPU index[③], developed by Baker et al. (2015), is based on newspaper archives from *Access World New's NewsBank* service, which represents the U. S. market uncertainty in a greater range. Unlike using monthly uncertainty data in the other studies, we use daily VIX and EPU indices to capture high-frequency effects of U. S. market uncertainty, which provides more complete information on influence from exogenous shocks to stock markets, as indicated by Bolloverslev and Wright (2001) and Narayan and Sharma (2015).

The full sample covers the period from 2 January 2003 to 31 October 2017, and all holiday dates are excluded. We convert all stock prices and exogenous shock indices into daily logarithmic percentage return and change rate series.

3.3.2 Preliminary Analysis

Table 3.1 shows the descriptive statistics and the results of the unit

---

① The MSCI emerging markets ex Asia index includes: Brazil, Chile, Colombia, Czech Republic, Egypt, Greece, Hungary, Mexico, Peru, Poland, Russia, Qatar, South Africa, Turkey, and United Arab Emirates.

② All daily VIX index is provided by Chicago Board Options Exchange (www. cboe. com).

③ All U. S. daily EPU index is provided by Economic Policy Uncertainty (www. policyuncertainty. com).

root test for stock return series. The average returns of the emerging Asian markets are relatively larger than those of global developed and other emerging markets, especially in China, India, and Thailand markets. Regarding risk, the standard deviations of most emerging Asian and other emerging stock returns are high, and the standard deviation of global developed stock return is low, indicating that developed stock markets are relatively stable.

Regarding non-normality, the distributions of all return series are negatively skewed, indicating that large negative returns are more frequent than large positive returns. Moreover, all return series show signs of significantly higher excess kurtosis with respect to the normal distribution, indicating the presence of peaked distributions and fat tails. Thus, the Jarque-Bera test statistics (Jarque and Bera, 1980) significantly reject the assumption of a normal distribution for all return series, supporting the use of the Student's t-distribution rather than the Gaussian distribution in the estimation process. Furthermore, the Ljung-Box (Ljung and Box, 1978) Q statistics clearly indicate some presence of a serial autocorrelation in the return residuals ($Q(30)$) and the squared residuals series ($Q^2(30)$) of all return series. By applying the ARCH test of Engle (1982), we strongly reject the null of no ARCH effects in all cases, implying that using a GARCH-family model is appropriate. As shown in Panel B of Table 3. 1, the return series for all considered markets are also found to be stationary processes, based on two unit root tests (i.e. the ADF and the PP test) and a stationarity test (the KPSS test).

Table 3. 2 presents the results of the long memory (LM) tests for squared returns (as a proxy variable of volatility) of stock markets. We consider four types of LM test procedures, namely, the Hurst – Mandelbrot

Table 3.1 **Descriptive statistics and unit root tests**

	China	Korea	Taiwan Area	Hong Kong SAR	Singapore	India	Malaysia	Thailand	World	EM_ex_Asia
Panel A: Descriptive statistics										
Mean	0.0466	0.0378	0.0232	0.0319	0.0278	0.0467	0.0208	0.0458	0.0244	0.0291
Max.	14.044	24.987	8.2315	10.449	8.5634	19.486	5.7838	10.521	9.0967	11.306
Min.	−12.836	−20.672	−7.1661	−12.567	−9.8093	−12.041	−11.279	−18.084	−7.325	−13.612
SD	1.6835	1.7775	1.3717	1.2491	1.2558	1.6459	0.9508	1.5534	0.9838	1.5115
Skewness	−0.0627	−0.2011	−0.2220	−0.1990	−0.2339	−0.0764	−0.4076	−0.6535	−0.5016	−0.5249
Kurtosis	7.2849	19.194	3.2768	8.4196	6.1277	9.7788	8.4901	10.694	10.137	8.4932
J-B	8540.2 ***	59295 ***	1759.1 ***	11430 ***	6075.9 ***	15388 ***	11703 ***	18671 ***	16693 ***	11782 ***
$Q(30)$	98.032 ***	67.332 ***	105.78 ***	63.629 ***	109.36 ***	109.94 ***	98.696 ***	63.248 ***	123.45 ***	158.24 ***
$Q^2(30)$	5633.1 ***	2748.9 ***	2181.8 ***	4993.2 ***	6526.5 ***	1334.0 ***	588.53 ***	1087.1 ***	8129.9 ***	7311.6 ***
ARCH(10)	130.18 ***	132.93 ***	47.618 ***	141.68 ***	152.31 ***	38.388 ***	23.459 ***	44.159 ***	178.48 ***	166.34 ***
Panel B: Unit root tests										
ADF	−59.778 ***	−60.445 ***	−59.272 ***	−60.818 ***	−60.645 ***	−57.908 ***	−55.443 ***	−60.706 ***	−44.130 ***	−53.970 ***
PP	−59.734 ***	−60.448 ***	−59.219 ***	−60.818 ***	−60.773 ***	−58.039 ***	−55.555 ***	−60.741 ***	−55.147 ***	−53.619 ***
KPSS	0.2047	0.1066	0.0571	0.0877	0.2111	0.2196	0.3316	0.1696	0.0959	0.4587

Notes: The J-B corresponds to the test statistic for the null hypothesis of normality in the sample returns distribution. The Ljung-Box statistic, $Q(30)$, and $Q^2(30)$ check for serial autocorrelation in the residuals and the squared residuals up to the 30th order, respectively. The ARCH (10) test of Engle (1982) is used to check for the presence of ARCH effects. In the case of Panel B, MacKinnon's 1% critical value is −3.435 for the augmented Dickey and Fuller (ADF; 1979) and Phillips and Perron (PP; 1988) tests. The critical value for the Kwiatkowski, Phillips, Schmidt, and Shim (KPSS; 1992) test is 0.739 at the 1% significance level. *** indicates a rejection of the null hypothesis at the 1% significance level.

Table 3.2 Long memory tests for squared returns of stock markets

	China	Korea	Taiwan Area	Hong Kong SAR	Singapore	India	Malaysia	Thailand	World	EM_ex_Asia
Panel A: Hurst-Mandelbrot R/S test										
Test statistic	6.6307 ***	4.3244 ***	5.5765 ***	6.2037 ***	6.9922 ***	5.5517 ***	4.4581 ***	4.0722 ***	6.6798 ***	5.4904 ***
Panel B: Lo R/S test										
$q=1$	5.9210 ***	4.1600 ***	5.3522 ***	5.2961 ***	6.3619 ***	5.1404 ***	4.2576 ***	3.6033 ***	6.0135 ***	5.0078 ***
$q=5$	4.1885 ***	3.3805 ***	4.2462 ***	3.8327 ***	4.4032 ***	4.2481 ***	3.4991 ***	2.9733 ***	4.2657 ***	3.5852 ***
Panel C: GSP test										
$d\ (m=T/16)$	0.5385 ***	0.6540 ***	0.3950 ***	0.5273 ***	0.5484 ***	0.3427 ***	0.2426 ***	0.3076 ***	0.6389 ***	0.7432 ***
	(0.0322)	(0.0322)	(0.0322)	(0.0322)	(0.0322)	(0.0322)	(0.0322)	(0.0322)	(0.0322)	(0.0322)
$d\ (m=T/32)$	0.4544 ***	0.5094 ***	0.4470 ***	0.4208 ***	0.4640 ***	0.3426 ***	0.2585 ***	0.2998 ***	0.6115 ***	0.6546 ***
	(0.0455)	(0.0455)	(0.0455)	(0.0455)	(0.0455)	(0.0455)	(0.0455)	(0.0455)	(0.0455)	(0.0455)
$d\ (m=T/64)$	0.4212 ***	0.3731 ***	0.5805 ***	0.3611 ***	0.3985 ***	0.3253 ***	0.3431 ***	0.2435 ***	0.4183 ***	0.3599 ***
	(0.0645)	(0.0645)	(0.0645)	(0.0645)	(0.0645)	(0.0645)	(0.0645)	(0.0645)	(0.0645)	(0.0645)
Panel D: GPH test										
$d\ (m=T^{0.5})$	0.4334 ***	0.3748 ***	0.6435 ***	0.3363 ***	0.4313 ***	0.2592 ***	0.3481 ***	0.2628 ***	0.4630 ***	0.3803 ***
	(0.0910)	(0.0910)	(0.0910)	(0.0910)	(0.0910)	(0.0910)	(0.0910)	(0.0910)	(0.0910)	(0.0910)
$d\ (m=T^{0.6})$	0.5432 ***	0.4588 ***	0.4310 ***	0.4669 ***	0.5350 ***	0.3264 ***	0.2288 ***	0.3229 ***	0.6329 ***	0.7039 ***
	(0.0575)	(0.0575)	(0.0575)	(0.0575)	(0.0575)	(0.0575)	(0.0575)	(0.0575)	(0.0575)	(0.0575)
$d\ (m=T^{0.7})$	0.4205 ***	0.5409 ***	0.3140 ***	0.3854 ***	0.5200 ***	0.3058 ***	0.2148 ***	0.2408 ***	0.6278 ***	0.6794 ***
	(0.0370)	(0.0370)	(0.0370)	(0.0370)	(0.0370)	(0.0370)	(0.0370)	(0.0370)	(0.0370)	(0.0370)

Notes: The critical values of the Hurst—Mandelbrot R/S test and Lo R/S analyses are 2.098 at the 1% significance level, respectively. 'q' in the Lo R/S test is the number of autocorrelation lags. 'm' denotes the bandwidth for the GSP and the GPH tests. The numbers in the parentheses are the standard deviations of the estimates. *** indicates significance at the 1% level.

R/S test, the Lo R/S test, the Gaussian semi-parametric (GSP) test of Robinson and Henry (1999), and the GPH test of Geweke and Porter-Hudak (1983). As a result, the LM property is found to be highly significant for all squared return series, providing important evidence to support adopting a fractionally integrated GARCH model.

3.4 Empirical Results

In this section, we present the estimation results obtained from the ARMA-cDCC-FIEGARCH model, with and without exogenous shocks. Moreover, we provide the results of the VaR analysis and hedging effectiveness and the potential effect of exogenous shocks on them.

3.4.1 The ARMA-cDCC-FIEGARCH Model, without and with Exogenous Shocks

Table 3.3 presents the estimation results of the ARMA-cDCC-FIEGARCH model without exogenous shocks.① In panel A of the Table 3.3, the AR(1) parameter is significant for four out of ten cases under consideration, implying that past return information is instantaneously and rapidly embodied in current stock prices. Moreover, the fractional

① Here, we choose the appropriate lag order of the ARMA and ARCH process in the return and variance equations to better capture the features of the cDCC-FIEGARCH model. Specifically, we select the ARMA(1, 0)-cDCC-FIEGARCH(1, d, 1) model for the Singapore market and the ARMA(1, 1)-cDCC-FIEGARCH(1, d, 2) model for the Malaysia market, and the ARMA(1, 1)-cDCC-FIEGARCH(1, d, 1) model for other remaining markets.

integrated coefficients (d) are significant at the 1% level for all markets, implying the presence of high persistence. Furthermore, the leverage effect coefficient (λ_1) is negative and significant for all stock markets, except the China market, indicating that negative shocks have a stronger effect on conditional volatility than positive shocks for the same magnitude. The presence of both long memory and asymmetry features in conditional variance confirms that using the FIEGARCH specification is appropriate.

The estimation results of the cDCC model are reported in Panel B and C of Table 3. 3. We observe that the average correlations between the emerging Asian and global developed markets are relatively smaller than those between the emerging Asian and other global emerging markets. This result indicates that investors have better opportunities to diversify their assets when they choose the portfolio comprised of emerging Asian and global developed stock assets. In other words, the hedging role of developed markets is superior to that of other global emerging markets for all emerging Asian stock markets. Moreover, both the ARCH effect (α_{cDCC}) and GARCH effect (β_{cDCC}) are positive and significant for most markets, suggesting that the cDCC model provides a good fit. Additionally, the coefficients of the Student's t density function (df) are highly significant, which is consistent with the evidence reported in Table 3. 1 and supports the choice of the Student-t distribution.

Table 3. 4 provides the estimation results of the ARMA-cDCC-FIEGARCH model with exogenous shocks. We find that almost all VIX variables are positive and statistically significant, highlighting the importance of including this unscheduled news related to exogenous shocks in modelling time-varying correlations. In contrast, almost all

Table 3.3 Empirical results for the ARMA-cDCC-FIEGARCH model without exogenous shocks

	China	Korea	Taiwan Area	Hong Kong SAR	Singapore	India	Malaysia	Thailand	World	EM_ex_Asia
Panel A: Results of ARMA-FIEGARCH model										
Const. (M)	0.0749	0.0333 *	0.0124	0.0510 ***	0.0257 *	0.0707 ***	0.0486 ***	0.0800 ***	0.0192 **	0.0682 ***
	(0.0503)	(0.0201)	(0.0170)	(0.0141)	(0.0141)	(0.0229)	(0.0175)	(0.0242)	(0.0076)	(0.0248)
AR(1)	0.0310	0.6314 *	0.1884	0.1453	0.0393 **	0.5111 ***	0.2124	0.2751	0.0269	0.1978 *
	(0.9409)	(0.3483)	(0.3523)	(0.5169)	(0.0165)	(0.1669)	(0.2155)	(0.1859)	(0.1404)	(0.1010)
MA(1)	0.0332	−0.6185 *	−0.1368	−0.0787		−0.4164 **	−0.0888	−0.1940	0.0861	−0.0508
	(0.9676)	(0.3593)	(0.3615)	(0.5196)		(0.1743)	(0.2217)	(0.1834)	(0.1413)	(0.1014)
Const. (V)	1.4352 ***	1.5012 ***	1.3476 ***	0.8064 ***	0.8275 ***	1.0372 ***	0.5377	1.5075 ***	−0.0776	0.4968
	(0.2970)	(0.3073)	(0.2872)	(0.2544)	(0.3207)	(0.2612)	(0.3590)	(0.3405)	(0.2268)	(0.3127)
d-FIGARCH	0.5650 ***	0.5492 ***	0.6039 ***	0.5945 ***	0.5136 ***	0.4948 ***	0.6422 ***	0.6142 ***	0.5400 ***	0.5147 ***
	(0.0678)	(0.0972)	(0.0510)	(0.0804)	(0.0889)	(0.0510)	(0.0807)	(0.0525)	(0.0508)	(0.1102)
ARCH	1.6045	−0.3602	0.6465	0.3758	−0.2766	0.0104	0.8052	−0.0735	−0.2233	−0.4564 *
	(1.8849)	(0.2671)	(1.0702)	(1.1456)	(0.3043)	(0.2883)	(1.4865)	(0.3006)	(0.2330)	(0.2649)
GARCH	0.5946 ***	0.8369 ***	0.5739 ***	0.6001 *	0.8527 ***	0.6565 ***	0.3902	0.0702	0.7481 ***	0.7841 ***
	(0.1071)	(0.1002)	(0.2217)	(0.3444)	(0.0677)	(0.0985)	(1.2740)	(0.4747)	(0.0780)	(0.1586)
EGARCH(λ_1)	−0.0158	−0.0738 ***	−0.0474 *	−0.0470 **	−0.0479 ***	−0.0991 ***	−0.0469 ***	−0.1477 **	−0.1226 ***	−0.1118 ***
	(0.0144)	(0.0266)	(0.0272)	(0.0217)	(0.0176)	(0.0289)	(0.0178)	(0.0597)	(0.0348)	(0.0273)
EGARCH(λ_2)	0.0665	0.1038 ***	0.0634 **	0.0915 ***	0.1295 ***	0.1765 ***	0.1483 ***	0.3568 ***	0.1059 ***	0.1765 ***
	(0.0437)	(0.0277)	(0.0289)	(0.0354)	(0.0352)	(0.0339)	(0.0389)	(0.1142)	(0.0210)	(0.0300)

Continued

	China	Korea	Taiwan Area	Hong Kong SAR	Singapore	India	Malaysia	Thailand	World	EM_ex_Asia
Panel B: Results of cDCC between the emerging Asian and global developed stock markets										
$\rho_{Asia\text{-}DM}$	0. 1872	0. 3061 ***	0. 2604 ***	0. 3235 ***	0. 3696 ***	0. 2490 **	0. 1881	0. 2864 ***		
	(0. 1447)	(0. 0223)	(0. 0244)	(0. 0163)	(0. 0814)	(0. 1155)	(0. 1577)	(0. 0417)		
α_{cDCC}	0. 0058 ***	0. 0081 **	0. 0040 *	0. 0290 **	0. 0097 ***	0. 0056 ***	0. 0063 **	0. 0074 *		
	(0. 0022)	(0. 0042)	(0. 0024)	(0. 0128)	(0. 0030)	(0. 0018)	(0. 0029)	(0. 0043)		
β_{cDCC}	0. 9938 ***	0. 9749 ***	0. 9881 ***	0. 7557 ***	0. 9881 ***	0. 9932 ***	0. 9917 ***	0. 9875 ***		
	(0. 0023)	(0. 0187)	(0. 0078)	(0. 1383)	(0. 0036)	(0. 0027)	(0. 0060)	(0. 0120)		
df	8. 3347 ***	9. 1336 ***	8. 5887 ***	8. 3324 ***	8. 4656 ***	8. 4757 ***	7. 3117 ***	7. 3494 ***		
	(0. 7006)	(0. 8448)	(0. 7518)	(0. 7028)	(0. 7225)	(0. 6976)	(0. 5145)	(0. 5352)		
Panel C: Results of cDCC between the emerging Asian and other global emerging stock markets										
$\rho_{Asia\text{-}EM}$	0. 4018 ***	0. 3476 ***	0. 3080 ***	0. 3469 ***	0. 4448 ***	0. 3090 **	0. 3399 ***	0. 3421 ***		
	(0. 0155)	(0. 0165)	(0. 0141)	(0. 0176)	(0. 0594)	(0. 1351)	(0. 0444)	(0. 0206)		
α_{cDCC}	0. 0172 **	0. 0035	0. 0000	0. 0217 ***	0. 0084 **	0. 0048	0. 0050 **	0. 0319 ***		
	(0. 0081)	(0. 0026)	(0. 0000)	(0. 0081)	(0. 0039)	(0. 0036)	(0. 0022)	(0. 0088)		
β_{cDCC}	0. 8844 ***	0. 9793 ***	0. 7499 *	0. 8815 ***	0. 9888 ***	0. 9942 ***	0. 9923 ***	0. 8950 ***		
	(0. 0507)	(0. 0121)	(0. 4536)	(0. 0322)	(0. 0063)	(0. 0056)	(0. 0040)	(0. 0354)		
df	8. 5100 ***	9. 7908 ***	8. 9603 ***	8. 3961 ***	9. 1803 ***	8. 3610 ***	7. 4333 ***	7. 7130 ***		
	(0. 7051)	(0. 9056)	(0. 7812)	(0. 6853)	(0. 8200)	(0. 6485)	(0. 5180)	(0. 5727)		

Continued

	China	Korea	Taiwan Area	Hong Kong SAR	Singapore	India	Malaysia	Thailand	World	EM_ex_Asia
Panel D: Diagnostic tests										
$Q(30)$	61. 488	18. 508	54. 317	48. 039	61. 357	42. 381	31. 586	38. 922	37. 970	32. 377
	[0. 0006]	[0. 9497]	[0. 0042]	[0. 0196]	[0. 0006]	[0. 0664]	[0. 3870]	[0. 1275]	[0. 1505]	[0. 3502]
$Q^2(30)$	27. 173	37. 970	47. 657	33. 258	40. 267	40. 197	10. 694	18. 347	24. 690	33. 866
	[0. 6142]	[0. 1505]	[0. 0214]	[0. 3114]	[0. 0100]	[0. 1011]	[0. 9995]	[0. 9526]	[0. 7400]	[0. 2862]
$log\ (L)$	-6769. 0	-6898. 2	-6242. 1	-5604. 9	-5531. 7	-6656. 5	-4745. 9	-6635. 4	-4339. 1	-6284. 3
$log\ (L)_{Asia\text{-}DM}$	-10742	-10919	-10316	-9596. 7	-9307. 2	-10605	-8730. 4	-10608		
$log\ (L)_{Asia\text{-}EM}$	-12562	-12816	-12224	-11491	-11144	-12448	-10568	-12472		

Notes: The standard errors are in parentheses and the p-values are in brackets. ***, **, and * indicate rejection of the null hypothesis at the 1%, 5%, and 10% significance levels, respectively.

Table 3. 4 Empirical results for the ARMA-cDCC-FIEGARCH model with exogenous shocks

	China	Korea	Taiwan Area	Hong Kong SAR	Singapore	India	Malaysia	Thailand	World	EM_ex_Asia
Panel A: Results of ARMA-FIEGARCH model										
Const. (M)	0. 0807 ***	0. 0378 *	0. 0217	0. 0549 **	0. 0325 ***	0. 0854 ***	0. 0506 ***	0. 0938 ***	0. 0734 ***	0. 1351 ***
	(0. 0171)	(0. 0212)	(0. 0182)	(0. 0219)	(0. 0121)	(0. 0227)	(0. 0161)	(0. 0213)	(0. 0108)	(0. 0295)
AR(1)	-0. 1157 ***	0. 6214 *	0. 1147	0. 1413	0. 0339 ***	0. 4907 ***	0. 2167	0. 2299	-0. 2324 *	0. 1180
	(0. 0265)	(0. 3666)	(0. 3161)	(0. 6253)	(0. 0082)	(0. 1690)	(0. 2131)	(0. 1475)	(0. 1191)	(0. 1211)
MA(1)	0. 1782 ***	-0. 6101	-0. 0712	-0. 0770		-0. 3994 **	-0. 0978	-0. 1554	0. 3271 ***	0. 0153
	(0. 0255)	(0. 3763)	(0. 3227)	(0. 6355)		(0. 1753)	(0. 2188)	(0. 1446)	(0. 1148)	(0. 1324)
Const. (V)	1. 4193 ***	1. 5022 ***	1. 3559 ***	0. 8058 ***	0. 8240 **	1. 0143 ***	0. 5211	1. 4477 ***	-0. 1525	0. 1164
	(0. 2818)	(0. 3219)	(0. 2873)	(0. 2735)	(0. 3199)	(0. 2721)	(0. 3470)	(0. 3211)	(0. 3030)	(0. 4348)
VIX	0. 0068 *	0. 0056	0. 0152 ***	0. 0058	0. 0096 **	0. 0140 ***	0. 0078 *	0. 0120 ***	0. 0284 ***	0. 0200 ***
	(0. 0039)	(0. 0043)	(0. 0042)	(0. 0040)	(0. 0044)	(0. 0045)	(0. 0043)	(0. 0041)	(0. 0038)	(0. 0040)
EPU	-0. 0001	0. 0005	0. 0008 *	0. 0006	0. 0001	-0. 0001	-0. 0009	0. 0008	-0. 0005	0. 0002
	(0. 0005)	(0. 0005)	(0. 0005)	(0. 0005)	(0. 0005)	(0. 0007)	(0. 0006)	(0. 0007)	(0. 0004)	(0. 0005)
d-FIGARCH	0. 5670 ***	0. 5541 ***	0. 6235 ***	0. 6049 ***	0. 5232 ***	0. 5017 ***	0. 6394 ***	0. 6169 ***	0. 6379 ***	0. 5814 ***
	(0. 0665)	(0. 1044)	(0. 0453)	(0. 0705)	(0. 0855)	(0. 0478)	(0. 0865)	(0. 0506)	(0. 0486)	(0. 0844)
ARCH	1. 7960	-0. 3360	1. 1058	0. 5114	-0. 2160	0. 0222	0. 7780	-0. 0900	-0. 2306	-0. 3536
	(1. 9874)	(0. 2908)	(1. 4018)	(0. 9949)	(0. 3494)	(0. 2836)	(1. 5564)	(0. 2079)	(0. 3556)	(0. 4442)
GARCH	0. 5836 ***	0. 8329 ***	0. 4704 **	0. 5560 **	0. 8411 ***	0. 6503 ***	0. 4224	0. 0690	0. 6067 ***	0. 6455 **
	(0. 1072)	(0. 1119)	(0. 2270)	(0. 2700)	(0. 0724)	(0. 0935)	(1. 3381)	(0. 3377)	(0. 2152)	(0. 3106)
EGARCH(λ_1)	-0. 0152	-0. 0719 ***	-0. 0432	-0. 0460 **	-0. 0462 ***	-0. 1011 ***	-0. 0481 ***	-0. 1502 ***	-0. 1728 ***	-0. 1332 ***
	(0. 0139)	(0. 0253)	(0. 0275)	(0. 0217)	(0. 0174)	(0. 0287)	(0. 0176)	(0. 0558)	(0. 0312)	(0. 0273)
EGARCH(λ_2)	0. 0628	0. 1019 ***	0. 0580 **	0. 0886 **	0. 1232 ***	0. 1769 ***	0. 1493 ***	0. 3625 ***	0. 1426 ***	0. 1849 ***
	(0. 0418)	(0. 0274)	(0. 0293)	(0. 0344)	(0. 0364)	(0. 0336)	(0. 0380)	(0. 1094)	(0. 0199)	(0. 0274)

Continued

	China	Korea	Taiwan Area	Hong Kong SAR	Singapore	India	Malaysia	Thailand	World	EM_ex_Asia
Panel B: Results of cDCC between the emerging Asian and global developed stock markets										
$\rho_{Asia\text{-}DM}$	0.3350 ***	0.3113 ***	0.2661 ***	0.3275 ***	0.3969 ***	0.2511	0.2607 ***	0.2991 ***		
	(0.0158)	(0.0207)	(0.0147)	(0.0162)	(0.0660)	(0.1729)	(0.0248)	(0.0314)		
α_{cDCC}	0.0279 *	0.0080	0.0000	0.0339 **	0.0087 ***	0.0048 **	0.0138	0.0068		
	(0.0145)	(0.0050)	(0.0000)	(0.0146)	(0.0031)	(0.0019)	(0.0187)	(0.0088)		
β_{cDCC}	0.7546 ***	0.9722 ***	0.7030	0.7257 ***	0.9887 ***	0.9943 ***	0.9622 ***	0.9864 ***		
	(0.1674)	(0.0258)	(2.5637)	(0.1573)	(0.0043)	(0.0037)	(0.0812)	(0.0298)		
df	9.4251 ***	10.434 ***	10.061 ***	9.3344 ***	9.4219 ***	9.5447 ***	7.8997 ***	8.0065 ***		
	(0.8944)	(1.0731)	(1.0085)	(0.8724)	(0.8789)	(0.8768)	(0.5989)	(0.6389)		
Panel C: Results of cDCC between the emerging Asian and other global emerging stock markets										
$\rho_{Asia\text{-}EM}$	0.4048 ***	0.3498 ***	0.3077 ***	0.3497 ***	0.4493 ***	0.2795 **	0.3506 ***	0.3451 ***		
	(0.0153)	(0.0160)	(0.0140)	(0.0175)	(0.0568)	(0.1258)	(0.0380)	(0.0203)		
α_{cDCC}	0.0189 **	0.0030	0.0000	0.0231 ***	0.0077 **	0.0039	0.0050 **	0.0327 ***		
	(0.0090)	(0.0026)	(0.0000)	(0.0085)	(0.0038)	(0.0028)	(0.0022)	(0.0088)		
β_{cDCC}	0.8672 ***	0.9795 ***	0.7659 *	0.8752 ***	0.9896 ***	0.9956 ***	0.9919 ***	0.8895 ***		
	(0.0611)	(0.0143)	(0.4153)	(0.0330)	(0.0062)	(0.0041)	(0.0041)	(0.0355)		
df	8.9401 ***	10.432 ***	9.7665 ***	8.8235 ***	9.7220 ***	8.8158 ***	7.6423 ***	8.0550 ***		
	(0.7909)	(1.0428)	(0.9340)	(0.7623)	(0.9355)	(0.7365)	(0.5489)	(0.6309)		

Continued

	China	Korea	Taiwan Area	Hong Kong SAR	Singapore	India	Malaysia	Thailand	World	EM_ex_Asia
Panel D: Diagnostic tests										
$Q(30)$	58. 364	21. 791	52. 846	46. 534	59. 365	42. 362	31. 742	36. 877	38. 963	29. 430
	[0. 0014]	[0. 8615]	[0. 0062]	[0. 0276]	[0. 0011]	[0. 0667]	[0. 3796]	[0. 1808]	[0. 1266]	[0. 4951]
$Q^2(30)$	28. 332	48. 673	47. 538	34. 000	39. 992	43. 243	12. 556	18. 342	29. 182	55. 137
	[0. 5528]	[0. 0170]	[0. 0220]	[0. 2808]	[0. 1050]	[0. 0558]	[0. 9979]	[0. 9527]	[0. 5080]	[0. 0034]
$log\ (L)$	-6767. 8	-6895. 1	-6226. 7	-5601. 4	-5525. 8	-6643. 7	-4739. 7	-6625. 0	-4239. 2	-6248. 2
$log\ (L)_{Asia-DM}$	-10672	-10850	-10250	-9523. 5	-9234. 8	-10531	-8665. 9	-10536		
$log\ (L)_{Asia-EM}$	-12532	-12788	-12190	-11458	-11111	-12412	-10539	-12440		

Note: See Table 3. 3 notes.

EPU variables are insignificant, implying that shocks from the U. S. stock market have a greater influence on global stock markets by comparison with U. S. economic policy uncertainty. This result indicates that transmission mechanism between the uncertainty of stock markets is stronger due to the globalization of financial markets. Interestingly, we observe that the values of fractional integrated coefficients are higher for the model, including exogenous shocks in volatility, which is similar to the study of Mensi et al. (2015a). Moreover, we find that the model with exogenous shocks in Table 3. 4 reduces the values of all GARCH parameters (β), which indicates a significant decrease in the degree of volatility persistence. This finding is consistent with studies by Hammoudeh and Li (2008), Wang and Moore (2009), Mensi et al. (2015b), and Dong and Yoon (2018), in which they consider structural breaks in volatility processes via Inclán and Tiao's (1994) ICSS algorithm. Hence, controlling exogenous shocks can also address the problem that the degree of volatility persistence is overestimated in the GARCH model (Aggarwal et al., 1999; Lamoureux and Lastrapes, 1990). Additionally, if we consider these exogenous shocks, we obtain larger average correlation coefficients ($\rho_{Asia\text{-}DM}$ and $\rho_{Asia\text{-}EM}$), implying that exogenous shocks lead to higher relationships between the stock markets.

Finally, in Panel D of Tables 3. 3 and 3. 4, we evaluate the accuracy of the model specifications using a common diagnostic test. The insignificance of the Ljung - Box $Q(30)$ and $Q^2(30)$ tests shows no serial correlations in the standardized residuals and the squared standardized residuals series at the conventional levels, except for few cases, indicating that the cDCC-FIEGARCH model, with and without exogenous shocks, is well specified. Moreover, the higher values of the log likelihood [$\log(L)$, $\log(L)_{Asia\text{-}DM}$, and $\log(L)_{Asia\text{-}EM}$] indicate that the model with exogenous shocks is superior to its counterpart without exogenous shocks for all stock markets. Thus, we conclude that this model specification is the best to capture the relationships between emerging Asian and other global stock markets.

Figure 3. 1 displays a visual representation of the shifts in the cDCCs between the emerging Asian and other global developed and emerging stock markets using the ARMA-cDCC-FIEGARCH model, with and without exogenous shocks, over the daily sample period. Figure 3. 1 shows significant variability in the conditional correlations across all pairs, which indicates that investors should frequently adjust their active portfolio strategies according to variable market conditions. Moreover, the results of the cDCCs show that the many relationships between the emerging Asian and other global stock markets increase during the global financial crisis (GFC). This finding indicates that investors have limited opportunities to diversify their assets during this period, especially in the Southeast and South Asian markets, which is consistent with studies by Kenourgios and Dimitriou (2015) and Kim et al. (2015). Finally, we find small differences in the cDCCs for the model, with and without exogenous shocks. Hence, considering exogenous shocks might improve the accuracy of hedging strategy computations, which we subsequently discuss.

3. 4. 2 The VaR Analysis

Tables 3. 5 to 3. 7 report the one-day-ahead VaR performance results calculated by the normal, Student-t, and skewed Student-t FIEGARCH models, with and without exogenous shocks for MSCI China, world,

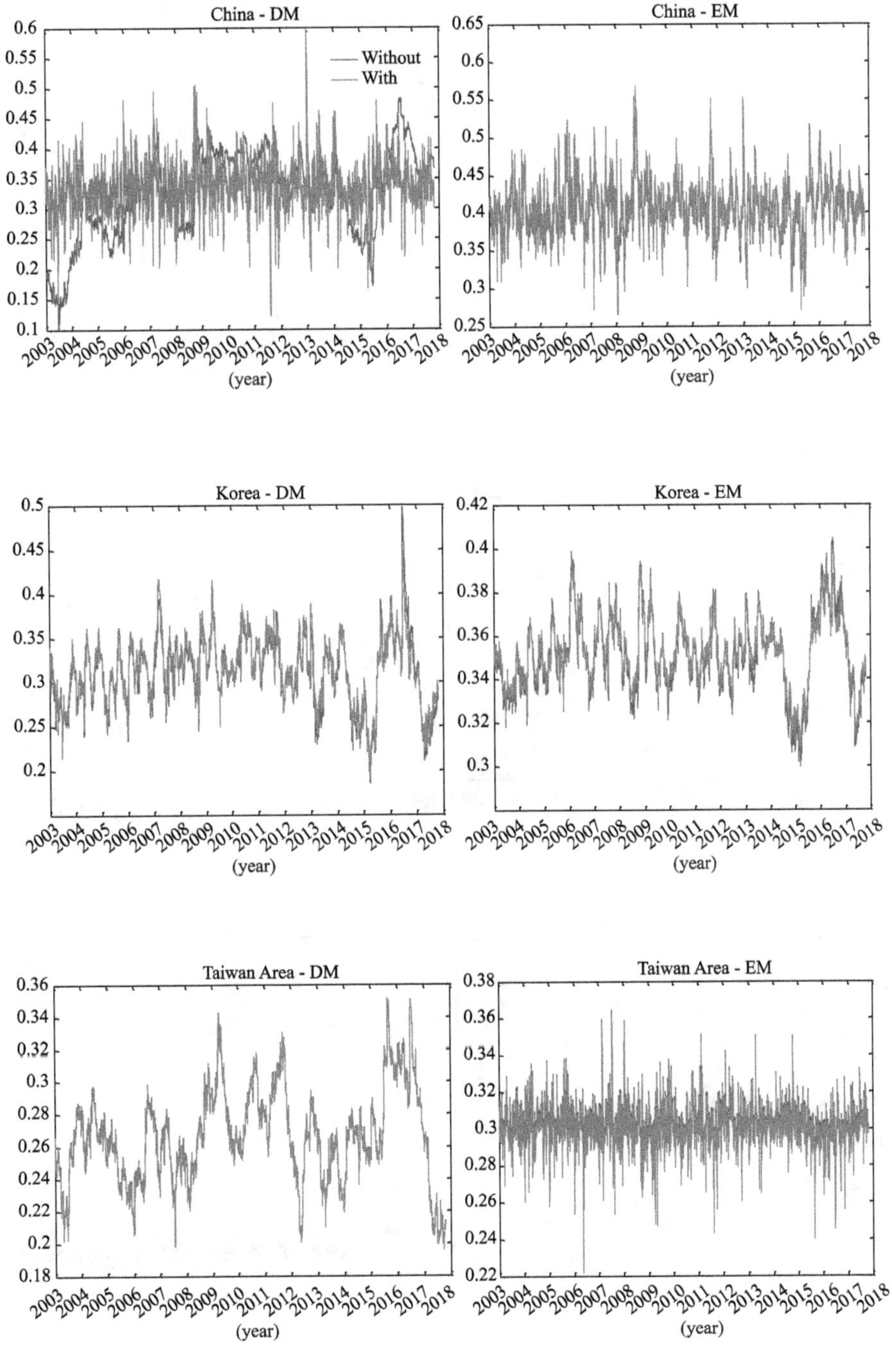
China - DM
Without
With
(year)
China - EM
(year)
Korea - DM
(year)
Korea - EM
(year)
Taiwan Area - DM
(year)
Taiwan Area - EM
(year)

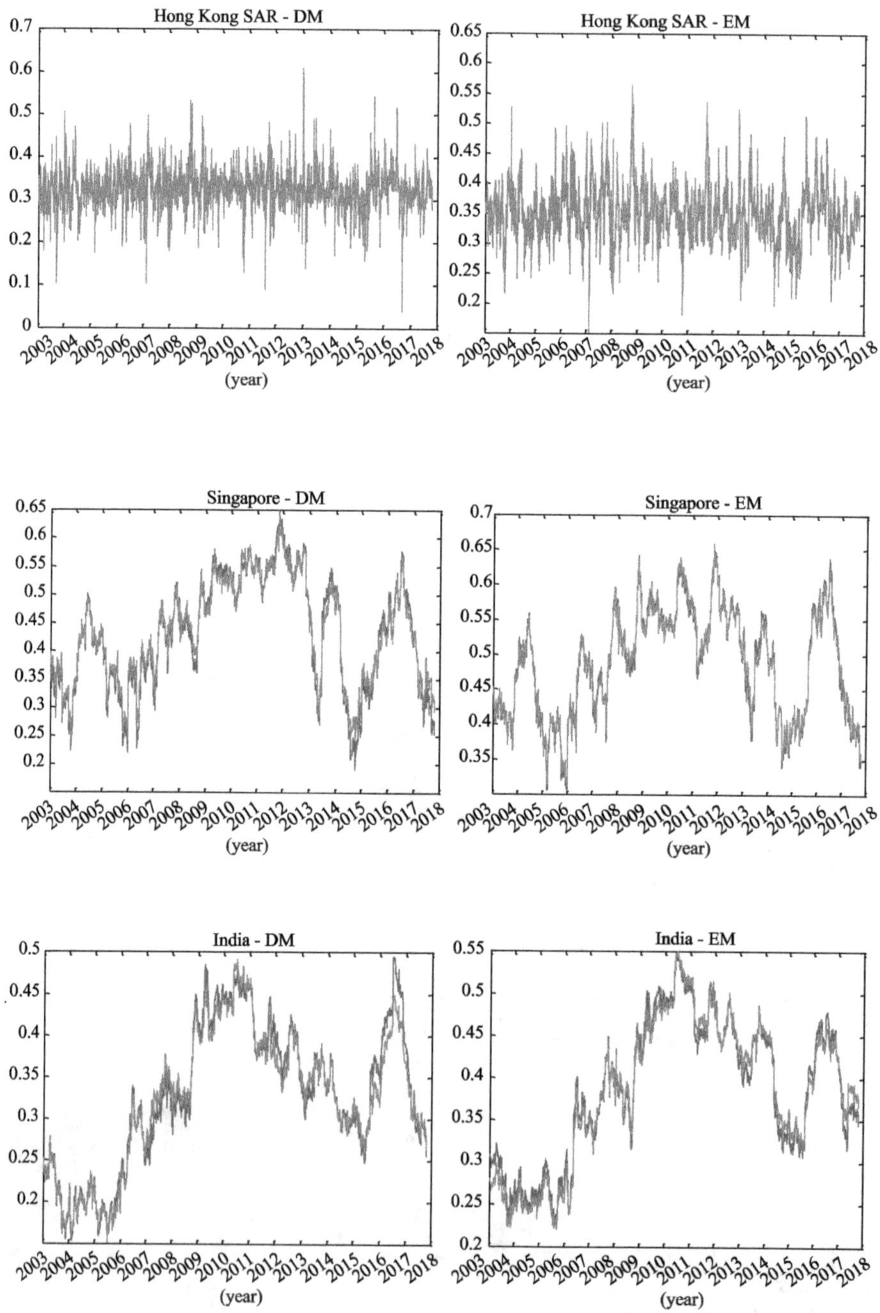
Hong Kong SAR - DM
(year)
Hong Kong SAR - EM
(year)
Singapore - DM
(year)
Singapore - EM
(year)
India - DM
(year)
India - EM
(year)

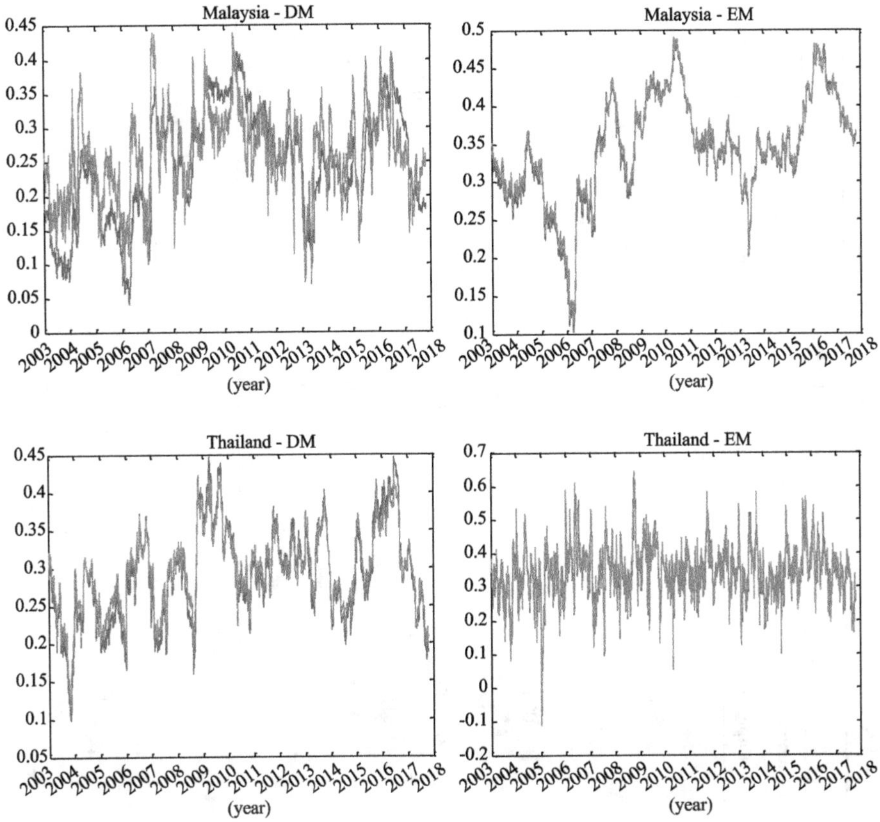

Figure 3. 1 Time-varying cDCCs, with and without exogenous shocks

and emerging markets ex Asia indices, respectively. We evaluate the VaR performance results at different significance levels ranging from 0. 05 to 0. 0025, and Kupiec LR test is applied to assess the accuracy of the VaR models. More specifically, the VaR models provide a good performance if the null hypothesis that the empirical failure rate is equal to prescribed quantiles is not rejected, otherwise these models present a poor performance.

Table 3. 5 **VaR analysis for MSCI China index**

Quantile	Without exogenous shocks				With exogenous shocks			
	Short positions		Long positions		Short positions		Long positions	
	Failure rate	Kupiec LRT	Failure rate	Kupiec LRT	Failure rate	Kupiec LRT	Failure rate	Kupiec LRT
Panel A: FIEGARCH model with normal distribution								
0. 9500/ 0. 0500	0. 9578	5. 1866 ** [0. 0228]	0. 0588	5. 9636 ** [0. 0146]	0. 9576	4. 8699 ** [0. 0273]	0. 0580	4. 9442 ** [0. 0262]
0. 9750/ 0. 0250	0. 9764	0. 3306 [0. 5653]	0. 0352	14. 721 ** [0. 0001]	0. 9752	0. 0035 [0. 9527]	0. 0347	13. 298 ** [0. 0003]
0. 9900/ 0. 0100	0. 9878	1. 7222 [0. 1894]	0. 0192	25. 831 ** [0. 0000]	0. 9878	1. 7135 [0. 1905]	0. 0186	23. 212 ** [0. 0000]
0. 9950/ 0. 0050	0. 9915	8. 0443 ** [0. 0046]	0. 0140	42. 015 ** [0. 0000]	0. 9917	6. 9826 ** [0. 0082]	0. 0137	39. 924 ** [0. 0000]
0. 9975/ 0. 0025	0. 9943	11. 593 ** [0. 0007]	0. 0083	32. 140 ** [0. 0000]	0. 9943	11. 580 ** [0. 0007]	0. 0091	39. 615 ** [0. 0000]
Panel B: FIEGARCH model with Student-t distribution								
0. 9500/ 0. 0500	0. 9560	3. 0384 [0. 0813]	0. 0616	10. 241 ** [0. 0014]	0. 9544	1. 6500 [0. 1990]	0. 0616	10. 241 ** [0. 0014]
0. 9750/ 0. 0250	0. 9801	4. 3683 ** [0. 0366]	0. 0305	4. 5582 ** [0. 0328]	0. 9788	2. 3758 [0. 1232]	0. 0287	2. 1100 [0. 1463]

Continued

Quantile	Without exogenous shocks				With exogenous shocks			
	Short positions		Long positions		Short positions		Long positions	
	Failure rate	Kupiec LRT	Failure rate	Kupiec LRT	Failure rate	Kupiec LRT	Failure rate	Kupiec LRT
Panel B: FIEGARCH model with Student-t distribution								
0. 9900/	0. 9912	0. 5841	0. 0124	2. 1315	0. 9917	1. 2207	0. 0119	1. 3385
0. 0100		[0. 4447]		[0. 1443]		[0. 2692]		[0. 2473]
0. 9950/	0. 9959	0. 6075	0. 0034	2. 3461	0. 9959	0. 6075	0. 0039	1. 0499
0. 0050		[0. 4357]		[0. 1256]		[0. 4357]		[0. 3055]
0. 9975/	0. 9987	2. 7377	0. 0010	4. 2718 **	0. 9987	2. 7377	0. 0010	4. 2718 **
0. 0025		[0. 0980]		[0. 0388]		[0. 0980]		[0. 0388]
Panel C: FIEGARCH model with skewed Student-t distribution								
0. 9500/	0. 9557	2. 7526	0. 0585	5. 6257 **	0. 9542	1. 4431	0. 0603	8. 1863 **
0. 0500		[0. 0971]		[0. 0177]		[0. 2296]		[0. 0042]
0. 9750/	0. 9785	2. 0389	0. 0285	1. 8475	0. 9785	2. 0389	0. 0277	1. 1269
0. 0250		[0. 1533]		[0. 1741]		[0. 1533]		[0. 2884]
0. 9900/	0. 9912	0. 5793	0. 0114	0. 7273	0. 9915	0. 8660	0. 0117	1. 0143
0. 0100		[0. 4466]		[0. 3938]		[0. 3521]		[0. 3139]
0. 9950/	0. 9959	0. 6040	0. 0034	2. 3396	0. 9961	1. 0454	0. 0036	1. 6207
0. 0050		[0. 4370]		[0. 1261]		[0. 3066]		[0. 2030]
0. 9975/	0. 9987	2. 7328	0. 0010	4. 2659 **	0. 9987	2. 7328	0. 0010	4. 2659 **
0. 0025		[0. 0983]		[0. 0389]		[0. 0983]		[0. 0389]

Notes: The critical value of the Kupiec LPT statistic is 3. 84 at the 5% significant level. The *p*-values are in brackets. ** indicates a rejection of the null hypothesis at the 5% significance level.

Table 3. 6 **VaR analysis for MSCI world index**

Quantile	Without exogenous shocks				With exogenous shocks			
	Short positions		Long positions		Short positions		Long positions	
	Failure rate	Kupiec LRT	Failure rate	Kupiec LRT	Failure rate	Kupiec LRT	Failure rate	Kupiec LRT
Panel A: FIEGARCH model with normal distribution								
0. 9500/ 0. 0500	0. 9591	7. 1219 ** [0. 0076]	0. 0546	1. 7075 [0. 1913]	0. 9456	1. 5249 [0. 2169]	0. 0484	0. 2016 [0. 6534]
0. 9750/ 0. 0250	0. 9803	4. 8233 ** [0. 0281]	0. 0350	14. 022 ** [0. 0002]	0. 9710	2. 4218 [0. 1197]	0. 0228	0. 7954 [0. 3725]
0. 9900/ 0. 0100	0. 9925	2. 6436 [0. 1040]	0. 0186	23. 247 ** [0. 0000]	0. 9881	1. 3463 [0. 2459]	0. 0080	1. 6246 [0. 2025]
0. 9950/ 0. 0050	0. 9961	1. 0454 [0. 3066]	0. 0101	15. 561 ** [0. 0000]	0. 9922	5. 0898 ** [0. 0241]	0. 0039	1. 0454 [0. 3066]
0. 9975/ 0. 0025	0. 9977	0. 0452 [0. 8316]	0. 0065	16. 949 ** [0. 0000]	0. 9959	3. 4874 [0. 0618]	0. 0023	0. 0452 [0. 8316]
Panel B: FIEGARCH model with Student-t distribution								
0. 9500/ 0. 0500	0. 9580	5. 5478 ** [0. 0185]	0. 0572	4. 0779 ** [0. 0434]	0. 9412	5. 9636 ** [0. 0146]	0. 0464	1. 1020 [0. 2938]
0. 9750/ 0. 0250	0. 9834	12. 733 ** [0. 0004]	0. 0321	7. 3699 ** [0. 0066]	0. 9713	2. 1254 [0. 1449]	0. 0179	8. 9248 ** [0. 0028]
0. 9900/ 0. 0100	0. 9956	15. 452 ** [0. 0000]	0. 0119	1. 3463 [0. 2459]	0. 9896	0. 0500 [0. 8231]	0. 0044	15. 452 ** [0. 0000]

Continued

Quantile	Without exogenous shocks				With exogenous shocks			
	Short positions		Long positions		Short positions		Long positions	
	Failure rate	Kupiec LRT	Failure rate	Kupiec LRT	Failure rate	Kupiec LRT	Failure rate	Kupiec LRT
Panel B: FIEGARCH model with Student-t distribution								
0. 9950/ 0. 0050	0. 9982	10. 447 ** [0. 0012]	0. 0049	0. 0049 [0. 9444]	0. 9956	0. 2883 [0. 5913]	0. 0018	10. 447 ** [0. 0012]
0. 9975/ 0. 0025	0. 9995	9. 0239 ** [0. 0027]	0. 0023	0. 0452 [0. 8316]	0. 9964	1. 7214 [0. 1895]	0. 0010	4. 2659 ** [0. 0389]
Panel C: FIEGARCH model with skewed Student-t distribution								
0. 9500/ 0. 0500	0. 9529	0. 6781 [0. 4102]	0. 0526	0. 5313 [0. 4661]	0. 9446	2. 3154 [0. 1281]	0. 0549	1. 9002 [0. 1681]
0. 9750/ 0. 0250	0. 9772	0. 7954 [0. 3725]	0. 0280	1. 3481 [0. 2456]	0. 9733	0. 4361 [0. 5090]	0. 0243	0. 0683 [0. 7938]
0. 9900/ 0. 0100	0. 9946	9. 7235 ** [0. 0018]	0. 0096	0. 0688 [0. 7931]	0. 9896	0. 0500 [0. 8231]	0. 0065	5. 5366 ** [0. 0186]
0. 9950/ 0. 0050	0. 9977	6. 9011 ** [0. 0086]	0. 0041	0. 6040 [0. 4370]	0. 9953	0. 0907 [0. 7633]	0. 0023	6. 9011 ** [0. 0086]
0. 9975/ 0. 0025	0. 9985	1. 6030 [0. 2055]	0. 0018	0. 8085 [0. 3686]	0. 9964	1. 7214 [0. 1895]	0. 0010	4. 2659 ** [0. 0389]

Note: See Table 3. 5 notes.

Table 3.7 **VaR analysis for MSCI emerging markets ex Asia index**

Quantile	Without exogenous shocks				With exogenous shocks			
	Short positions		Long positions		Short positions		Long positions	
	Failure rate	Kupiec LRT	Failure rate	Kupiec LRT	Failure rate	Kupiec LRT	Failure rate	Kupiec LRT
Panel A: FIEGARCH model with normal distribution								
0.9500/	0.9573	4.5027 **	0.0603	8.1863 **	0.9523	0.4534	0.0578	4.6685 **
0.0500		[0.0338]		[0.0042]		[0.5007]		[0.0307]
0.9750/	0.9793	3.0784	0.0344	12.670 **	0.9757	0.0683	0.0334	10.154 **
0.0250		[0.0793]		[0.0004]		[0.7938]		[0.0014]
0.9900/	0.9928	3.2562	0.0179	19.584 **	0.9891	0.2923	0.0148	7.7162 **
0.0100		[0.0711]		[0.0000]		[0.5888]		[0.0055]
0.9950/	0.9946	0.1454	0.0098	14.170 **	0.9935	1.5440	0.0070	2.7410
0.0050		[0.7030]		[0.0002]		[0.2140]		[0.0978]
0.9975/	0.9969	0.5310	0.0073	23.032 **	0.9961	2.5374	0.0049	7.0621 **
0.0025		[0.4662]		[0.0000]		[0.1112]		[0.0079]
Panel B: FIEGARCH model with Student-t distribution								
0.9500/	0.9562	3.2863	0.0637	14.120 **	0.9498	0.0049	0.0578	4.6685 **
0.0500		[0.0699]		[0.0002]		[0.9441]		[0.0307]
0.9750/	0.9827	10.356 **	0.0337	10.759 **	0.9762	0.2210	0.0295	3.0696
0.0250		[0.0013]		[0.0010]		[0.6383]		[0.0798]
0.9900/	0.9943	8.5434 **	0.0119	1.3463	0.9925	2.6436	0.0075	2.6436
0.0100		[0.0035]		[0.2459]		[0.1040]		[0.1040]

Continued

Quantile	Without exogenous shocks				With exogenous shocks			
	Short positions		Long positions		Short positions		Long positions	
	Failure rate	Kupiec LRT	Failure rate	Kupiec LRT	Failure rate	Kupiec LRT	Failure rate	Kupiec LRT
Panel B: FIEGARCH model with Student-t distribution								
0. 9950/ 0. 0050	0. 9974	5. 4769 ** [0. 0193]	0. 0062	1. 0648 [0. 3021]	0. 9969	3. 2129 [0. 0731]	0. 0041	0. 6040 [0. 4370]
0. 9975/ 0. 0025	0. 9990	4. 2659 ** [0. 0389]	0. 0039	2. 5374 [0. 1112]	0. 9977	0. 0452 [0. 8316]	0. 0023	0. 0452 [0. 8316]
Panel C: FIEGARCH model with skewed Student-t distribution								
0. 9500/ 0. 0500	0. 9518	0. 2742 [0. 6005]	0. 0562	3. 0122 [0. 0826]	0. 9487	0. 1325 [0. 7158]	0. 0570	3. 7970 [0. 0513]
0. 9750/ 0. 0250	0. 9788	2. 3604 [0. 1245]	0. 0290	2. 4218 [0. 1197]	0. 9764	0. 3306 [0. 5653]	0. 0287	2. 1254 [0. 1449]
0. 9900/ 0. 0100	0. 9933	4. 7000 ** [0. 0302]	0. 0093	0. 1823 [0. 6694]	0. 9925	2. 6436 [0. 1040]	0. 0070	3. 9408 ** [0. 0471]
0. 9950/ 0. 0050	0. 9966	2. 3396 [0. 1261]	0. 0044	0. 2883 [0. 5913]	0. 9969	3. 2129 [0. 0731]	0. 0041	0. 6040 [0. 4370]
0. 9975/ 0. 0025	0. 9990	4. 2659 ** [0. 0389]	0. 0031	0. 5310 [0. 4662]	0. 9977	0. 0452 [0. 8316]	0. 0023	0. 0452 [0. 8316]

Note: See Table 3. 5 notes.

According to Table 3. 5, we find that the FIEGARCH models, with exogenous shocks, outperform its counterpart without exogenous shocks for MSCI China index, as the null hypothesis is rejected in 14 out of 30 cases (the sum of short and long trading positions using three different distribution innovations) for the models without exogenous shocks and in 12 out of 30 cases for the models with exogenous shocks at the 5% significance level. Similar results are obtained for MSCI world and emerging markets ex Asia indices in Tables 3. 6 and 3. 7. ① The null hypothesis is rejected in 15 (14) out of 30 cases for the models without exogenous shocks and in 9 (6) out of 30 cases for the models with exogenous shocks for MSCI world (emerging markets ex Asia) index at the 5% significance level. Overall, we can conclude that the consideration of exogenous shocks in the ARMA-cDCC-FIEGARCH model provides more accurate forecasting results for short and long trading positions for the emerging Asian and other global stock markets, which can assist investors in avoiding the uncertainty in maximum losses and constructing a more suitable risk management strategy.

3. 4. 3 Portfolio Investment Analysis

Table 3. 8 presents the summary statistics for the optimal portfolio weights and hedge ratios obtained from the estimation results of the ARMA-cDCC-FIEGARCH model, without and with exogenous shocks. We find that the means of optimal portfolio weights of developed markets

---

① The results for the rest of the indices are similar to those for the three indices mentioned above. To save space, the results are not reported and are available on request.

are larger than those of other global emerging markets, indicating that investors should hold more of developed stock assets than other global emerging stock assets to minimize risk. The means of hedge ratios of other global emerging markets are larger than those of developed markets, implying that other global emerging markets have forced investors to pay more expensive hedging costs. More importantly, we observe a weak increase in all means of portfolio weights and a weak decrease in most means of hedge ratios after considering exogenous shocks for stock markets, which indicates that developed and other emerging stock markets can provide a more effective role in building hedging strategy.

Table 3.8 Summary statistics for the portfolio weights and hedge ratios

	Portfolio weight		Hedge ratio	
	Without exogenous shocks	With exogenous shocks	Without exogenous shocks	With exogenous shocks
Panel A: Results for global developed stock markets				
China—DM	0.8505 (0.1170)	0.8599 (0.1196)	0.1857 (0.0764)	0.1852 (0.0605)
Korea—DM	0.8690 (0.0858)	0.8758 (0.0908)	0.1669 (0.0498)	0.1650 (0.0485)
Taiwan Area—DM	0.7785 (0.1247)	0.7866 (0.1261)	0.1699 (0.0564)	0.1653 (0.0455)
Hong Kong SAR—DM	0.7083 (0.1445)	0.7197 (0.1504)	0.2421 (0.0702)	0.2403 (0.0731)
Singapore—DM	0.7303 (0.1700)	0.7426 (0.1780)	0.3287 (0.1180)	0.3253 (0.1116)
India—DM	0.8354 (0.1244)	0.8412 (0.1260)	0.1958 (0.0898)	0.1894 (0.0822)
Malaysia—DM	0.5503 (0.1840)	0.5650 (0.1903)	0.2384 (0.1206)	0.2454 (0.1034)
Thailand—DM	0.8117 (0.1414)	0.8212 (0.1397)	0.1756 (0.0786)	0.1744 (0.0727)

Continued

	Portfolio weight		Hedge ratio	
	Without exogenous shocks	With exogenous shocks	Without exogenous shocks	With exogenous shocks
Panel B: Results for other global emerging stock markets				
China—EM	0. 5884 (0. 2101)	0. 5945 (0. 2165)	0. 3721 (0. 1162)	0. 3722 (0. 1193)
Korea—EM	0. 6088 (0. 1924)	0. 6133 (0. 1997)	0. 3095 (0. 0913)	0. 3093 (0. 0945)
Taiwan Area—EM	0. 4990 (0. 1917)	0. 5018 (0. 1965)	0. 3195 (0. 0909)	0. 3186 (0. 0937)
Hong Kong SAR—EM	0. 3853 (0. 1848)	0. 3919 (0. 1939)	0. 4298 (0. 1335)	0. 4304 (0. 1372)
Singapore—EM	0. 3512 (0. 2251)	0. 3601 (0. 2361)	0. 6063 (0. 1810)	0. 6050 (0. 1866)
India—EM	0. 5647 (0. 2078)	0. 5690 (0. 2127)	0. 3709 (0. 1419)	0. 3689 (0. 1456)
Malaysia—EM	0. 2432 (0. 1564)	0. 2485 (0. 1625)	0. 5294 (0. 1809)	0. 5317 (0. 1805)
Thailand—EM	0. 5568 (0. 2257)	0. 5618 (0. 2291)	0. 3349 (0. 1467)	0. 3353 (0. 1479)

Note: The standard deviations are in the parentheses.

In the Appendices, appendix Figure 3. 1 presents time-varying hedging ratios, with and without exogenous shocks. We find the presence of small differences in hedging ratios with and without exogenous shocks, implying that controlling the impact from the U. S. market is necessary. Additionally, hedge ratios showed similar upward patterns during the GFC, meaning investors need to spend more on hedging costs during periods of market turbulence. Overall, Kroner and Ng (1998) indicate that estimating the right time-varying covariance matrix is essential for asset pricing and risk management. Thus, omitting the potential effect of exogenous shocks on stock markets in modelling time-varying correlations could lead to a worse portfolio strategy.

To assess the usefulness of employing exogenous shocks in building portfolios, we compare the quality of portfolios obtained from the ARMA-cDCC-FIEGARCH model, without and with exogenous shocks. Here, we consider two portfolios, namely, the optimally weighted portfolio (Portfolio I) constructed by using the method of Kroner and Ng (1998), and the portfolio (Portfolio II) whose weights are determined according to the method of Kroner and Sultan (1993).

We compute two hedging effectiveness measures. Following Ku et al. (2007), the variance reduction of the portfolios is assessed by comparing the percentage reduction in the variance of Portfolios I-II with respect to a single emerging Asian stock asset as:

$$Variance\ Reduction = 1 - \frac{Var_P}{Var_S} \tag{3.13}$$

where Var_P and Var_S are the variance of Portfolios I-II and single stock asset, and a higher value indicates a larger reduction in variance.

However, the variance reduction measure is appropriate when investors seek to minimize the variance. In practice, investors care more about downside risk than upside risk, making this measure inadequate for measuring risk. To address this problem, we estimate the lower partial moment (LPM). According to Cotter and Hanly (2012), the decreases in LPM can be used to compute a risk reduction measure:

$$LPM\ Reduction = 1 - \frac{LPM_{1\ P}}{LPM_{1\ S}} \tag{3.14}$$

where $LPM_{1\ P}$ and $LPM_{1\ S}$ represent the average loss below a target return of zero in the Portfolios I-II and single stock asset, respectively. We use $n = 1$ as the order of LPM, meaning that the investor is risk neutral.

Table 3.9 presents the hedging effectiveness measures for the

Table 3. 9 **Hedging effectiveness measures**

	Portfolio I				Portfolio II			
	Variance reduction		LPM reduction		Variance reduction		LPM reduction	
	Without exogenous shocks	With exogenous shocks	Without exogenous shocks	With exogenous shocks	Without exogenous shocks	With exogenous shocks	Without exogenous shocks	With exogenous shocks
Panel A: Results for global developed stock markets								
China—DM	0. 6691	0. 6748	0. 4184	0. 4317	0. 7243	0. 7267	0. 4759	0. 4831
Korea—DM	0. 6893	0. 6923	0. 4361	0. 4470	0. 7427	0. 7463	0. 4967	0. 5037
Taiwan Area—DM	0. 5736	0. 5757	0. 3486	0. 3576	0. 5489	0. 5496	0. 3781	0. 3824
Hong Kong SAR—DM	0. 4696	0. 4815	0. 2597	0. 2868	0. 4947	0. 5000	0. 2922	0. 3022
Singapore—DM	0. 4390	0. 4430	0. 2573	0. 2752	0. 5717	0. 5767	0. 3594	0. 3732
India—DM	0. 6609	0. 6607	0. 4174	0. 4221	0. 7186	0. 7206	0. 4628	0. 4692
Malaysia—DM	0. 3899	0. 4017	0. 2014	0. 2311	0. 1293	0. 1402	0. 0701	0. 0827
Thailand—DM	0. 6422	0. 6444	0. 4082	0. 4182	0. 6666	0. 6691	0. 4276	0. 4337
Panel B: Results for other global emerging stock markets								
China—EM	0. 3443	0. 3531	0. 1661	0. 1808	0. 4076	0. 4082	0. 1837	0. 1892
Korea—EM	0. 3937	0. 4056	0. 1986	0. 2149	0. 4221	0. 4251	0. 2020	0. 2070
Taiwan Srea—EM	0. 2755	0. 2756	0. 1294	0. 1332	−0. 0288	−0. 0304	0. 0109	0. 0124
Hong Kong SAR—EM	0. 1600	0. 1693	0. 0667	0. 0885	−0. 1409	−0. 1369	−0. 1282	−0. 1205
Singapore—EM	0. 0934	0. 0995	0. 0584	0. 0746	0. 0686	0. 0727	−0. 0099	−0. 0005
India—EM	0. 3582	0. 3606	0. 1784	0. 1839	0. 3678	0. 3674	0. 1588	0. 1625
Malaysia—EM	0. 1028	0. 1095	0. 0211	0. 0388	−1. 0241	−1. 0151	−0. 4400	−0. 4306
Thailand—EM	0. 3613	0. 3648	0. 1810	0. 1892	0. 2608	0. 2624	0. 1024	0. 1075

Portfolios I-II obtained from the model without and with exogenous shocks. The results reveal that the Asian-DM portfolios achieve higher values for two hedging effectiveness measures, indicating that inclusion of developed stock asset in the portfolios can assist investors more effectively in reducing volatility and downside risk. Moreover, we find that high value of variance reduction and LPM reduction are achieved for the China, Korea, India, and Thailand markets, indicating that investors, including other global stock assets in their portfolios could obtain better hedging effectiveness. Considering exogenous shocks, we also find a significant increase in the degree of hedging effectiveness for almost all portfolios, compared to the cases without exogenous shocks. This finding shows that incorporating exogenous shocks in our models can provide more accurate portfolio strategies.

3.5 Conclusions and Policy Implications

This study investigates the properties of the conditional volatilities and the time-varying correlations between emerging Asian and other global developed and emerging stock markets. For this purpose, we apply the ARMA-cDCC-FIEGARCH model, with and without exogenous shocks, to the eight emerging Asian and the two classified stock indices for the period spanning 2 January 2003 to 31 October 2017. Moreover, to evaluate the usefulness of incorporating exogenous shocks in modelling time-varying correlations, we compare the VaR analysis and hedging effectiveness using the results from the ARMA-cDCC-

FIEGARCH model, with and without exogenous shocks.

Our analysis confirms the presence of leverage effects and long memory property in the conditional volatility for almost all markets, emphasizing the importance of using the ARMA-cDCC-FIEGARCH model. The empirical results also show that the shocks from the U. S. stock market have a greater influence on global stock markets compared to that from U. S. economic policy. More importantly, we find that considering exogenous shocks reduces the degree of volatility persistence for all markets, thereby improving the accuracy of the ARMA-cDCC-FIEGARCH model, which plays the same role of controlling structural breaks via Inclán and Tiao's (1994) ICSS algorithm. Moreover, if we consider exogenous shocks in our models, we will obtain more accurate results for the VaR analysis and better hedging strategies. Additionally, we find that developed stock asset is a cheaper hedge asset than other global emerging stock asset, and Asian-DM portfolios can provide better hedging effectiveness. Finally, investors have limited opportunities to diversify their assets during GFC, as other global stock assets provide higher correlations and hedge ratios.

The findings of this study are of potential interest to international investors, researchers, and policymakers. First, researchers should pay more attention to the influence of exogenous shocks on stock markets when they create an econometric model to analyse economic issues, because incorporating exogenous shocks in their model could provide more accurate estimation results and more factual conclusions. Second, diversified portfolios comprising of emerging Asian and other global stock assets can reduce risk efficiently. However, it is obvious that hedging strategies depend on regular and extreme market conditions, investors should hold more of the other global stock assets during regular periods and hold more of the other safe haven assets during periods of turmoil. Third, since the risk spillover effect from U. S. stock market to other global stock markets is strong due to the globalization of financial markets, government needs to build a market mechanism to hedge against risk from the external market.

Chapter 4

Asymmetric Dependence Structures for Regional Stock Markets: An Unconditional Quantile Regression Approach

4.1 Introduction

According to the efficient market hypothesis (Fama, 1970, 1998), stock prices reflect all available information and investors are expected to act rationally. However, there are different market conditions in real stock markets, such as bear, normal, and bull markets. Investors' fear (greed) is more clearly exposed in bear (bull) markets than in normal markets; thus, extreme market conditions can lead to irrational decisions by investors because of herding behaviour, in which investor sentiment (Baker and Wurgler, 2006; Kumar and Lee, 2006; Shiller, 2015) overreacts to changes in stock prices and economic factors. Moreover, black swan events have occurred more frequently in recent years, while unexpected global and regional events often lead to huge crashes in global stock markets. In the above two processes, market crashes can happen immediately, whereas stock price rises take a long time (Ni et al., 2015), which provides evidence of the obvious asymmetric effects in stock markets.

Given the asymmetry of stock markets, this study investigates the dependence structures for six regional stock markets, considering different market conditions, mainly in bear or bull markets compared with normal markets. These regional stock markets include three developed (United States, Developed Europe, and Pacific) and three emerging (Asia, Emerging Europe, and Latin America) markets. Specifically, this study not only examines the dependence structures among six regional stock markets, but also explores the effect of global economic factors on them.

Building a diversified portfolio of multiple assets that are less relevant can reduce risk (Markowitz, 1952), which drives investors to diversify their assets across borders and regions, highlighting the importance of exploring the relationships among stock markets. Recently, a number of empirical studies have explored the relationships among stock markets by using different techniques, time periods, and samples. For example, Mensi et al. (2017) investigate the dynamic relationships and portfolio diversification between major developed and BRICS (Brazil, Russia, India, China, and South Africa) stock markets by applying both the dynamic conditional correlation-FIEGARCH and the dynamic equicorrelation-FIEGARCH models. Aloui and Hkiri (2014) examine the short-term and long-term comovements among Gulf Cooperation Council stock markets by using the wavelet coherence approach. By using both static and dynamic cointegration analysis, Guidi and Ugur (2014) examine whether south-eastern European stock markets were integrated with developed stock markets over 2000—2013. Based on constant and trend spillover models, Balli et al. (2015) study the return and volatility spillovers from developed stock markets to emerging Asia and Middle East and North Africa stock markets. However, although some studies explore the relationships among stock markets from various angles, few systematically capture global stock market relationships under bear, normal, and bull market conditions.

With the globalization of financial markets, stock markets are also increasingly affected by global economic factors. Moreover, the sign and intensity of the effect of global economic factors on stock markets may vary according to different stock market conditions. Our study selects

U. S. monetary policy, crude oil and gold prices, and U. S. financial stress as global economic factors. Many empirical studies show that monetary policy has asymmetric effects on stock markets (Jansen and Tsai, 2010; Laopodis, 2013; Li, 2015; Jareño et al., 2016). Jansen and Tsai (2010) examine the asymmetric impact of monetary policy on stock markets in bull and bear conditions. By using quantile regression, Jareño et al. (2016) indicate that the effect of the U. S. interest rate (IR) tends to be more pronounced in bear markets. Owing to the financialization of commodity markets, the asymmetric influence of crude oil prices on stock markets (Reboredo and Ugolini, 2016; You et al., 2017) and the safe haven property of gold (Baur and Lucey, 2010; Baur and McDermott, 2010) have received considerable attention from academic researchers and portfolio risk managers. Regarding financial stress, Reboredo and Uddin (2016) find that the effect of financial stress differs across commodity market return quantiles. Chen and Semmler (2018) study the spillover effects of financial markets and goods markets under both high and low financial stress regimes. In our study, we apply Chudik and Fratzscher's (2011) approach that uses the implied volatility of the S&P 500 index (VIX) and the TED spread to measure U. S. financial conditions.

From a methodological viewpoint, we use the quantile regression approach to capture the dependence structures for six regional stock markets, as this approach can provide the detailed dependence structures for different stock market conditions. The most commonly used quantile regression approach is the conditional quantile regression (CQR) method of Koenker and Bassett (1978). Indeed, owing to its flexibility and robustness, the CQR approach has been employed in many finance studies (e. g. Baur et al., 2012; Tsai, 2012; Baur, 2013; Mensi et al.,

2014; Jareño et al., 2016; Kocaarslan et al., 2017; You et al., 2017). However, in the CQR approach, the distributions are defined conditional on specific covariates, which may lead to inaccurate inferences and suboptimal implications for investors. To address the above limitation, we apply Firpo et al.'s (2009) unconditional quantile regression (UQR) approach instead of the traditional CQR approach because the distributions in the UQR approach are not influenced by specific covariates, but rather, by their entire distribution.

This study adds to and differs from existing studies in several aspects. First, Baur (2013) examines the dependence structures for groups of countries (e.g. G7, Eurozone, and Asian countries) by calculating their average coefficient estimates. Unlike previous studies, however, we focus on regional stock markets instead of individual stock markets. Because of the growing number of regional economic agreements (e.g. EU, NAFTA, ASEAN, MERCOSUR, Gulf Cooperation Council) and the current trend towards regional financial integration, such a regional insight can provide important information for global policymakers and investors (Guesmi and Nguyen, 2011; Kenourgios and Dimitriou, 2015). Second, we analyse both the dependence structures among and the effect of global economic factors on regional stock markets given the strengthening of both international investment and the globalization of financial markets. Unlike previous studies that only explore one of these aspects, we argue that selecting these two aspects for the analysis yields more comprehensive information. Third, this study selects five potential determinants as global economic factors, particularly U.S. monetary policy and the TED spread. Because of the dominance of the United States in the world economy, changes in its monetary policy affect the global economic situation, thereby influencing changes in global stock market prices. Moreover, the TED spread can reflect the fluctuations of investor sentiment and resulting changes in market liquidity. Finally, we apply the UQR approach, which has only previously been applied in economics fields such as labour economics (Firpo et al., 2009), health economics (Borah and Basu, 2013), and agricultural economics (Mishra et al., 2015). Introducing it into this research in the financial field thus provides more accurate extreme-value results and more useful implications.

The remainder of the paper is organized as follows. Section 2 provides the UQR framework. Section 3 describes our data, and Section 4 discusses the empirical results. Section 5 presents the conclusions.

4.2 Methodology

We use the quantile regression approach to explore the dependence structures for six regional stock markets. Compared with the classical linear regression model, this approach provides a more accurate and detailed result of the impact of conditional variables on the dependent variable (Koenker, 2005). The quantile regression approach that has pervaded the existing economic literature is the CQR approach first introduced by Koenker and Bassett (1978). The CQR approach of y_i given x_i is specified as follows:

$$Q_{y_i}(\tau \mid x_i) = x_i' \beta^{CQR}(\tau) \tag{4.1}$$

where $0 \leqslant \tau \leqslant 1$, y_i is each regional stock market return and $Q_{y_i}(\tau \mid x_i)$ denotes the τth conditional quantile of y_i. $\beta^{CQR}(\tau)$ determines the dependence relationship between vector x_i and the τth conditional quantile of y_i. Vector x_i is the other five regional stock market returns when focusing on the dependence structures among six regional stock markets, while it is the five global economic factors when focusing on their effects on regional stock markets. The coefficient $\beta^{CQR}(\tau)$ is estimated by minimizing the sum of the weighted absolute residuals between y_i and x_i (Koenker and Bassett, 1978; Koenker, 2005):

$$\hat{\beta}^{CQR}(\tau) = \text{argmin}[\sum_{y_i \geqslant x'\beta^{CQR}(\tau)} \tau \left| y_i - x_i'\beta^{CQR}(\tau) \right| + \sum_{y_i < x'\beta^{CQR}(\tau)} (1-\tau) \left| y_i - x_i'\beta^{CQR}(\tau) \right|]$$
$$= \text{argmin} \sum_{i=1}^{N} \rho_\tau [y_i - x_i'\beta^{CQR}(\tau)] \quad (4.2)$$

where $\rho_\tau(.)$ is the check function defined as $\rho_\tau(u) = u[\tau - I(u<0)]$. $I(.)$ is an indicator function and u is $y_i - x_i'\beta^{CQR}(\tau)$. The minimization problem is solved by using the linear programming methods proposed by Koenker and D'Orey (1987).

However, the distributions of the CQR approach are defined conditional on specific covariates. Further, the 95th percentile of the unconditional distribution of y may be different from the 95th percentile of the conditional distribution of y given x (Firpo et al., 2009). In particular, stock markets display the so-called extreme-value phenomenon because stock prices can rise or fall sharply. Therefore, their distribution based on specific covariates may be less than their complete distribution. Thus, if we apply the CQR approach, the interpretation of the coefficient estimates would change when different sets of covariates are considered. To address this problem, we use Firpo et al.'s (2009) UQR approach by using the concepts of the influence function (IF) and recentered influence function (RIF) widely applied in the robust statistics literature (Hampel et al., 2005). The IF can be written as follows:

$$IF(y; v, F_y) = \lim_{\varepsilon \to 0} \frac{\{v[(1-\varepsilon)F_y + \varepsilon G_y] - v(F_y)\}}{\varepsilon} \quad (4.3)$$

where $0 \leqslant \varepsilon \leqslant 1$, F_y denotes the cumulative distribution function of y, and G_y denotes the probability distribution that only puts mass at the value y. $v(F_y)$ is the value of a statistic. The RIF can be obtained by adding this statistic to its IF:

$$RIF(y; v, F_y) = v(F_y) + IF(y; v, F_y) \tag{4.4}$$

Firpo et al. (2009) show that a convenient feature of the RIF is that its expectation is equal to $v(F_y)$. Moreover, the conditional expectation of the $RIF(y; v, F_y)$ can be modelled as a function of the explanatory variables, that is, $E[RIF(y; v, F_y) \mid x] = m_v(x)$, which is an RIF regression model. When the statistic of interest is the τth quantile of the outcome distribution, $E[RIF(y; q_\tau, F_y) \mid x] = m_\tau(x)$ can be viewed as a UQR approach, and its RIF is specified as follows:

$$RIF(y; q_\tau, F_y) = q_\tau + IF(y; q_\tau, F_y) = q_\tau + (\tau - I\{y \leqslant q_\tau\})/f_y(q_\tau) \tag{4.5}$$

where q_τ is the τth quantile of the unconditional distribution of y and $q_\tau = v_\tau(F_y)$. $f_y(q_\tau)$ is the density of y evaluated at q_τ and $I(.)$ is an indicator function that takes the value one when the outcome variable, y, is less than q_τ, and 0 otherwise. The UQR estimator can be defined as the coefficient, $\beta^{UQR}(\tau)$, of the RIF of the explanatory variables, which is easily computed by using ordinary least squares regression:

$$RIF(y; q_\tau, F_y) = x'\beta^{UQR}(\tau) \tag{4.6}$$

In this study, we apply the UQR approach to investigate the dependence structures for regional stock markets. The advantage of this approach over the CQR approach is that the estimated effects are not influenced by the set of explanatory variables in the model, which helps us capture the more complete distribution of the outcome variable, thereby providing more accurate results for researchers and investors.

4.3 Data and Preliminary Analysis

4.3.1 Data

In this study, we consider daily stock price index series for six geographical regions: namely the United States, Developed Europe, Developed Pacific, Emerging Asia (EM_Asia), Emerging Europe (EM_Europe), and Emerging Latin America (EM_LA).[①] The data are extracted from the Morgan Stanley Capital Index database and all stock indices are denominated in U.S. dollars to avoid the effects of national currency fluctuations on the indices, as indicated by Bekaert and Harvey (1995) and Dimitriou et al. (2013).

Regarding economic factors, five potential global determinants are considered. Laopodis (2013) indicates that different monetary regimes have significant asymmetric effects on stock prices. This study selects the

① The Developed Europe index includes 15 markets: Austria, Belgium, Denmark, Finland, France, Germany, Ireland, Italy, Netherlands, Norway, Portugal, Spain, Sweden, Switzerland, and the United Kingdom. The Developed Pacific index includes five markets: Australia, Hong Kong SAR, Japan, New Zealand, and Singapore. The Emerging Asia index contains nine markets: China, India, Indonesia, Korea, Malaysia, Pakistan, Philippines, Taiwan Area, and Thailand. The Emerging Europe index contains six markets: Czech Republic, Greece, Hungary, Poland, Russia, and Turkey. The Emerging Latin America index contains five markets: Brazil, Chile, Colombia, Mexico, and Peru.

U. S. federal funds rate[①] to represent the IR, which can help academic researchers and investors understand how U. S. monetary policy influences stock markets. Since the financialization of commodity markets encourages investors to choose commodities as a hedge or safe haven, we consider the daily prices for two influential commodity markets, namely West Texas Intermediate (WTI) crude oil and gold.[②] To measure the risk and liquidity of a financial market, we also select the VIX index as a proxy for financial market risk and use the TED spread as a proxy for U. S. liquidity pressure.[③] The VIX measures the stock market's expectation of volatility implied by S&P 500 index options, which represents the uncertainty of the U. S. stock market. The TED spread is the difference between the three-month Eurodollar LIBOR (London Interbank Borrowing Rate) and three-month U. S. government debt (Treasury bill rate), with the increase in the TED spread indicating an increase in global credit risk. Given that Baker and Stein (2004) and Chau et al. (2016) respectively apply market liquidity (the turnover ratio) and the VIX to measure investor sentiment, the VIX and TED spread can also be considered to represent investor sentiment in our study.

The full sample covers the period from 2 January 2003 to 30 March 2018 and all holiday dates are excluded. We convert all stock prices and global economic factors into daily logarithmic percentage return and

---

① The federal funds rate is the effective funds rate as averages of daily rates and is collected from the Federal Reserve Bank of St. Louis (research. stlouisfed. org).

② All daily oil prices are provided by the Energy Information Administration (www. eia. gov) and all daily gold prices are provided by the World Gold Council (www. gold. org).

③ All daily VIX indices are provided by the Chicago Board Options Exchange (www. cboe. com) and all daily data for the TED spread are provided by the Federal Reserve Bank of St. Louis (research. stlouisfed. org).

change rate series.

4. 3. 2 Preliminary Analysis

Table 4. 1 shows the descriptive statistics and results of the unit root test for the return and change rate series. The average returns of emerging markets are larger than those of developed markets, whereas the standard deviations of developed markets are smaller than those of emerging markets, indicating that emerging stock markets have higher returns and higher risks than mature markets. Moreover, the global economic factors show high volatility, except for gold, implying that the uncertainty in the global financial market is large. Regarding non-normality, the distributions of all the stock return series are negatively skewed, indicating that large negative returns are more frequent than large positive returns for stock markets. This result provides evidence of the existence of asymmetry in stock markets, which supports the use of the UQR approach in our study. Furthermore, all the series exhibit signs of significantly higher excess kurtosis with respect to the normal distribution. Thus, the Jarque – Bera test statistics (Jarque and Bera, 1980) significantly reject the assumption of a normal distribution for all the return and change rate series.

As shown in Panel B of Table 4. 1, the return and change rate series for all the considered variables are also found to be stationary processes, except for the KPSS test for the EM_LA variable, based on two unit root tests (i.e. the ADF and PP tests) and a stationarity test (the KPSS test).

Table 4. 1 **Descriptive statistics and unit root tests**

	USA	Europe	Pacific	EM_Asia	EM_Europe	EM_LA	IR	WTI	Gold	VIX	TED
Panel A: Descriptive statistics											
Mean	0. 028	0. 018	0. 021	0. 036	0. 022	0. 038	0. 009	0. 019	0. 034	-0. 009	0. 031
Max.	11. 04	10. 70	9. 831	12. 65	18. 60	15. 36	90. 29	16. 41	6. 836	76. 83	74. 19
Min.	-9. 514	-10. 18	-9. 182	-8. 621	-19. 93	-15. 06	-78. 85	-13. 07	-9. 596	-35. 06	-69. 32
SD	1. 137	1. 340	1. 196	1. 279	1. 852	1. 735	9. 458	2. 313	1. 139	6. 921	7. 167
Skewness	-0. 380	-0. 195	-0. 390	-0. 346	-0. 466	-0. 431	0. 368	0. 034	-0. 372	1. 023	-0. 044
Kurtosis	15. 20	11. 48	8. 905	10. 51	15. 64	12. 61	26. 93	7. 362	8. 087	10. 95	13. 88
J-B	24705 ***	11917 ***	5869 ***	9397 ***	26581 ***	15409 ***	94819 ***	3149 ***	4372 ***	11148 ***	19593 ***
Panel B: Unit root tests											
ADF	-49. 28 ***	-30. 80 ***	-64. 98 ***	-56. 64 ***	-57. 47 ***	-57. 78 ***	-42. 35 ***	-66. 13 ***	-62. 67 ***	-49. 63 ***	-12. 93 ***
PP	-70. 14 ***	-63. 37 ***	-65. 27 ***	-56. 67 ***	-57. 30 ***	-57. 59 ***	-94. 43 ***	-66. 18 ***	-62. 67 ***	-81. 86 ***	-71. 00 ***
KPSS	0. 103	0. 134	0. 138	0. 146	0. 326	0. 475 **	0. 337	0. 147	0. 309	0. 045	0. 054

Notes: The J-B corresponds to the test statistic for the null hypothesis of normality in the sample returns distribution. MacKinnon's 1% critical value is -3. 435 for the augmented Dickey and Fuller (ADF; 1979) and Phillips and Perron (PP; 1988) tests. The critical value for the Kwiatkowski, Phillips, Schmidt, and Shim (KPSS; 1992) test is 0. 739 at the 1% significance level. *** and ** indicate a rejection of the null hypothesis at the 1% and 5% significance levels, respectively.

4.4 Empirical Results

In this section, we present the dependence structures among the six regional stock markets and asymmetric effects of the economic factors on these regional stock markets, using the UQR approach. Moreover, we also evaluate the results obtained from the UQR and CQR approaches.

4.4.1 Dependence Structures among the Regional Stock Markets

Figure 4.1 provides the UQR estimates for the dependence structures among the six regional stock markets. The blue line with hollow circles describes the 49 point estimates over the distribution of every two percentiles and the area between the red and green lines with multiplication signs indicates its corresponding 95% confidence interval. These results show that the relationships among regional stock markets are non-linear. We find a larger degree of dependence in the lower and upper quantiles than in the intermediate quantile for most stock markets, which is consistent with the study of Baur and McDermott (2010), who suggest that the relationships among financial markets are influenced by extreme market conditions. For instance, in the U. S. market, the relationship between the U. S. and Developed Europe (Emerging Latin America) stock markets shows an asymmetric u-shaped structure, indicating that these two regional stock market returns often simultaneously rise and fall during periods of extreme U. S. stock returns, especially extreme negative returns. However, the relationship between the U. S. and Developed Pacific (Emerging Asia and Emerging Europe) stock markets does not show this structure, implying that the contagion effect between the U. S. and Developed Europe (Emerging Latin America) stock markets is stronger than that between the U. S. and Developed Pacific (Emerging Asia and Emerging Europe) stock markets.

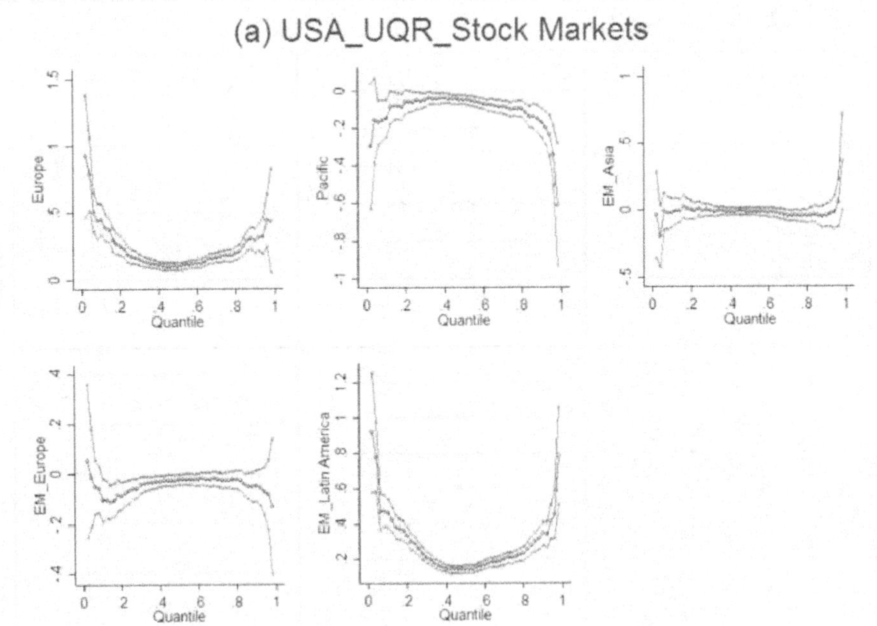

(b) Europe_UQR_Stock Markets

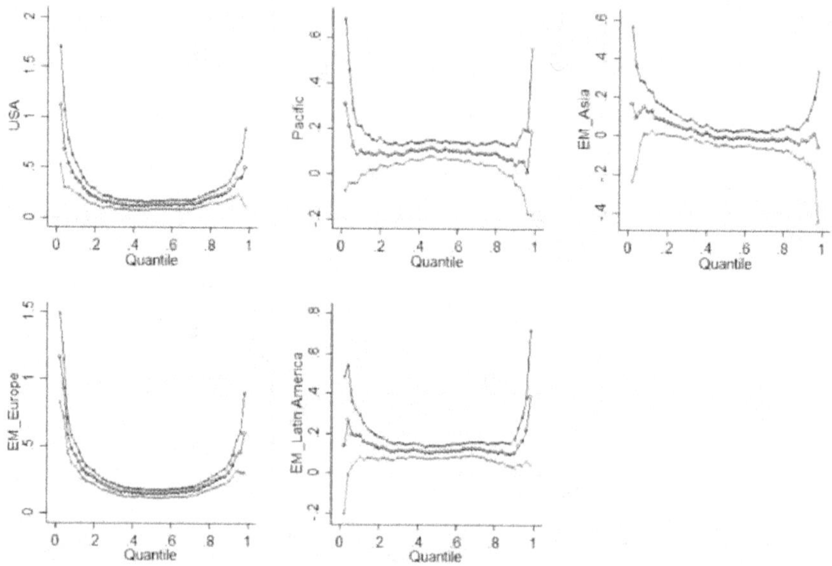

(c) Pacific_UQR_Stock Markets

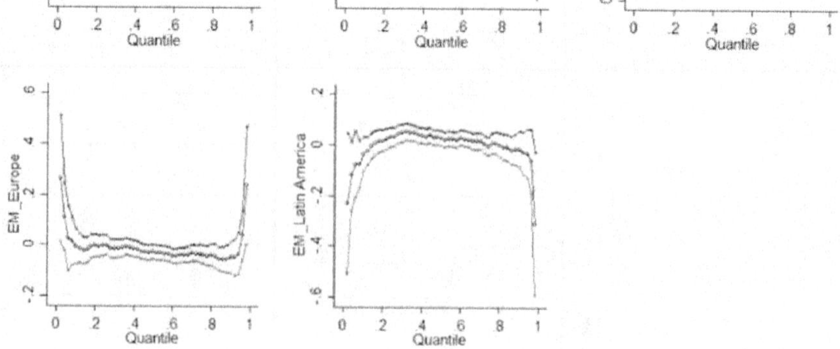

(d) EM_Asia_UQR_Stock Markets

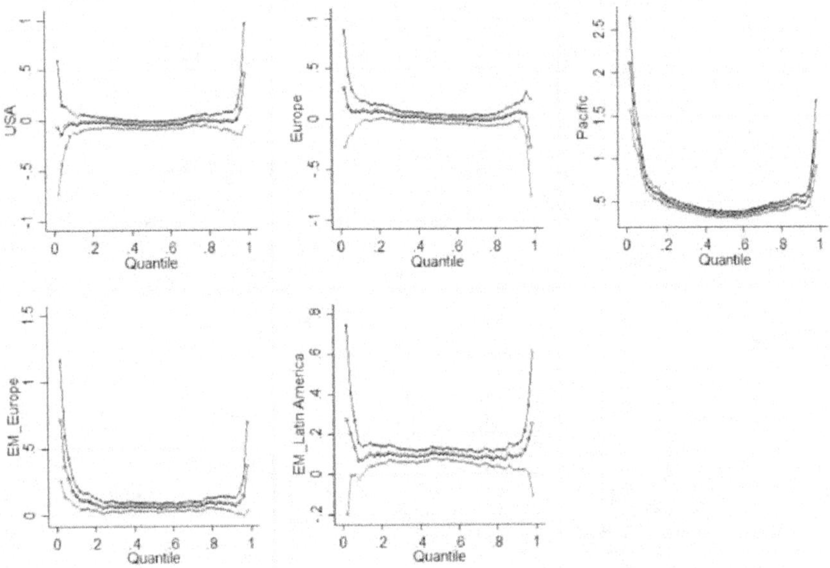

(e) EM_Europe_UQR_Stock Markets

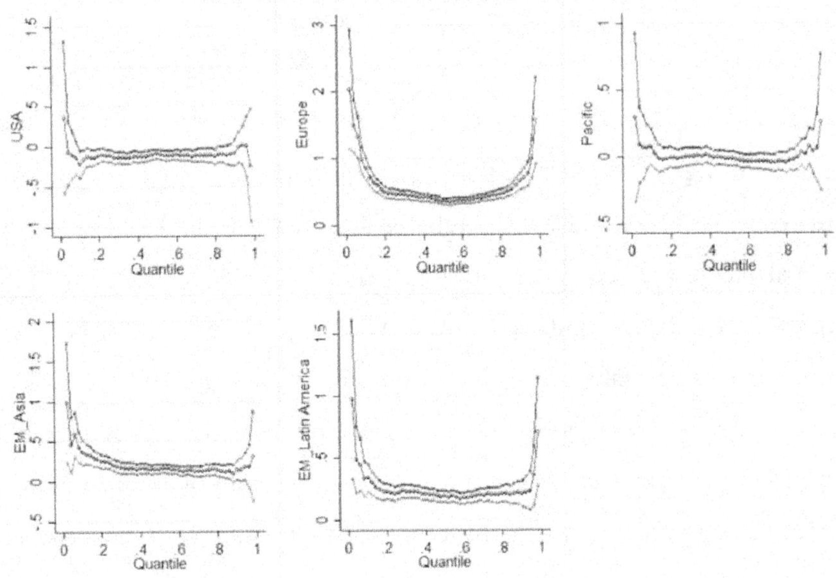

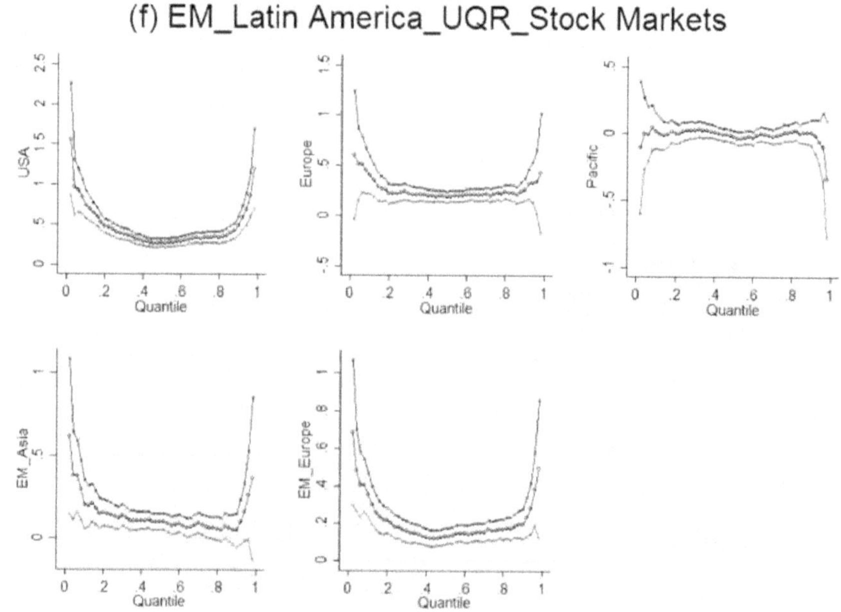

Figure 4. 1 UQR estimates for the dependence structures among the regional stock markets

Table 4. 2 reports the detailed UQR results for the U. S. stock market, using the other regional stock markets as the explanatory variable. ① To better analyse the relationship between the U. S. and other regional stock markets, we introduce Baur and McDermott's (2010) definition of a hedge and safe haven asset, in which a strong (weak) hedge and safe haven is an asset that is negatively correlated (uncorrelated) with another asset under regular and extreme market conditions, respectively. Most of the coefficients of the Developed Europe and Emerging Latin America stock markets are positive and

① To save space, the results for the other regional stock markets are not reported and are available on request.

significant for all quantiles of the U. S. market. By contrast, the coefficients of the Developed Pacific, Emerging Asia, and Emerging Europe stock markets are mostly significant and negative or insignificant, indicating that these three regional stock markets are a strong or weak hedge asset against the U. S. stock market in the different stock return quantiles. Since investors care more about downside risk than upside risk in the real world (Sortino and van der Meer, 1991; Cotter and Hanly, 2012), we need to pay attention to the dependence structure in the extreme negative stock return quantiles. We find that the coefficients of the Developed Pacific market are negative and significant in the 2%, 5%, and 10% stock return quantiles and that the coefficient of the Emerging Europe market is negative and significant in the 10% stock return quantile. The negative and significant coefficients indicate that these two regional stock markets are a strong safe haven asset against the U. S. stock market and provide an extra benefit to investors during periods of extreme negative U. S. stock returns. In addition, many of the coefficients of the Developed Pacific, Emerging Asia, and Emerging Europe stock markets are insignificant in the extreme negative stock return quantiles, meaning that these three regional stock markets are a weak safe haven asset against the U. S. stock market in these quantiles.

Table 4. 3 summarizes the relationships among the regional stock markets. The strong and weak relationships are reported in the middle and last columns, respectively. We observe that geographically and economically close stock markets exhibit a significant influence over each other, which is consistent with the finding of Johansson and Ljungwall (2009). For example, as both the U. S. and the Developed Europe stock markets are mature with advanced market mechanisms, their similar market structures lead to a high degree of correlation between them.

Table 4. 2 **UQR results for the U. S. stock market, using the other regional stock markets as the explanatory variable**

	Q(0. 01)	Q(0. 02)	Q(0. 05)	Q(0. 10)	Q(0. 50)	Q(0. 90)	Q(0. 95)	Q(0. 98)	Q(0. 99)
Europe	1. 434 ***	0. 928 ***	0. 619 ***	0. 451 ***	0. 098 ***	0. 290 ***	0. 375 ***	0. 438 **	1. 083
	(0. 537)	(0. 232)	(0. 099)	(0. 060)	(0. 013)	(0. 046)	(0. 082)	(0. 200)	(0. 741)
Pacific	-0. 490	-0. 296 *	-0. 159 **	-0. 147 ***	-0. 048 ***	-0. 174 ***	-0. 248 ***	-0. 613 ***	-1. 167 **
	(0. 354)	(0. 171)	(0. 079)	(0. 050)	(0. 012)	(0. 039)	(0. 065)	(0. 166)	(0. 554)
EM_Asia	0. 024	-0. 032	-0. 063	-0. 020	-0. 011	-0. 042	-0. 027	0. 363 **	0. 183
	(0. 337)	(0. 162)	(0. 086)	(0. 055)	(0. 013)	(0. 043)	(0. 072)	(0. 182)	(0. 587)
EM_Europe	0. 144	0. 052	-0. 062	-0. 104 **	-0. 024 **	-0. 049	-0. 083	-0. 133	-0. 395
	(0. 334)	(0. 158)	(0. 070)	(0. 044)	(0. 010)	(0. 032)	(0. 056)	(0. 137)	(0. 526)
EM_LA	1. 400 ***	0. 919 ***	0. 577 ***	0. 460 ***	0. 140 ***	0. 339 ***	0. 435 ***	0. 782 ***	2. 123 ***
	(0. 416)	(0. 174)	(0. 071)	(0. 042)	(0. 010)	(0. 034)	(0. 058)	(0. 141)	(0. 546)
Cons.	-3. 509 ***	-2. 633 ***	-1. 685 ***	-1. 143 ***	0. 036 ***	1. 120 ***	1. 568 ***	2. 286 ***	3. 050 ***
	(0. 198)	(0. 104)	(0. 054)	(0. 035)	(0. 010)	(0. 028)	(0. 042)	(0. 080)	(0. 240)

Notes: The standard errors are in parentheses. ***, **, and * indicate rejection of the null hypothesis at the 1%, 5%, and 10% significance levels, respectively.

Moreover, Latin America is geographically close to the United States and there is a lot of trade and investment between the United States and Latin America; thus, Latin America's economy is inextricably linked with that of the United States. Table 4.3 distinguishes the strong and weak relationships for each regional stock market, showing that a weak relationship between two regional markets has important implications for investors in terms of diversifying benefits.

Table 4.3 Summary relationships among each regional stock market

	Strong	Weak
USA	Europe, EM_LA	EM_Europe, EM_Asia, Pacific
Europe	USA, EM_Europe	EM_LA, Pacific, EM_Asia
Pacific	EM_Asia, Europe	EM_Europe, USA, EM_LA
EM_Asia	Pacific, EM_Europe	EM_LA, Europe, USA
EM_Europe	Europe, EM_Asia	EM_LA, USA, Pacific
EM_LA	USA, Europe	EM_Europe, EM_Asia, Pacific

4.4.2 Asymmetric Effects of Economic Factors on the Regional Stock Markets

Figure 4.2 illustrates the UQR estimates for the impact of the economic factors on the six regional stock markets. Similar to the results of Figure 4.1, the relationships among the regional stock markets and economic factors are also non-linear. Different monetary regimes affect increases and decreases in money supply, which then lead to changes in real output and stock prices. Jansen and Tsai (2010) show that the impact of monetary policy on stock markets in bear markets is large, negative, and statistically significant in the U.S. market. We find that the dependence structures among the regional stock markets and IR

(a) USA_UQR_Economic Factors

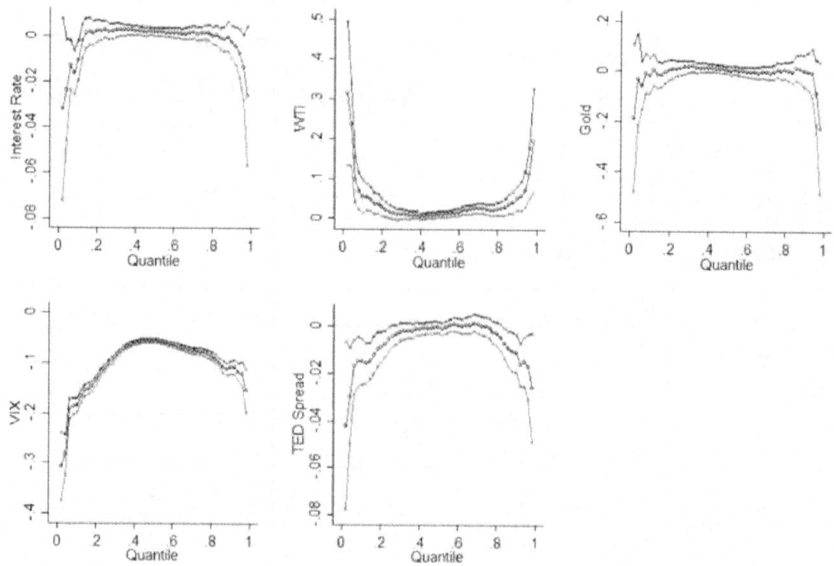

(b) Europe_UQR_Economic Factors

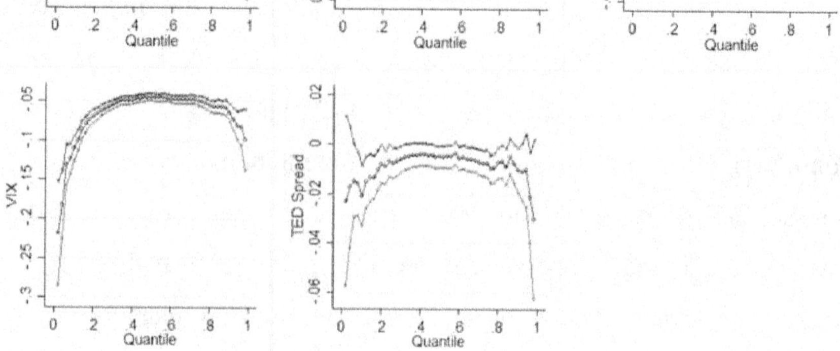

(c) Pacific_UQR_Economic Factors

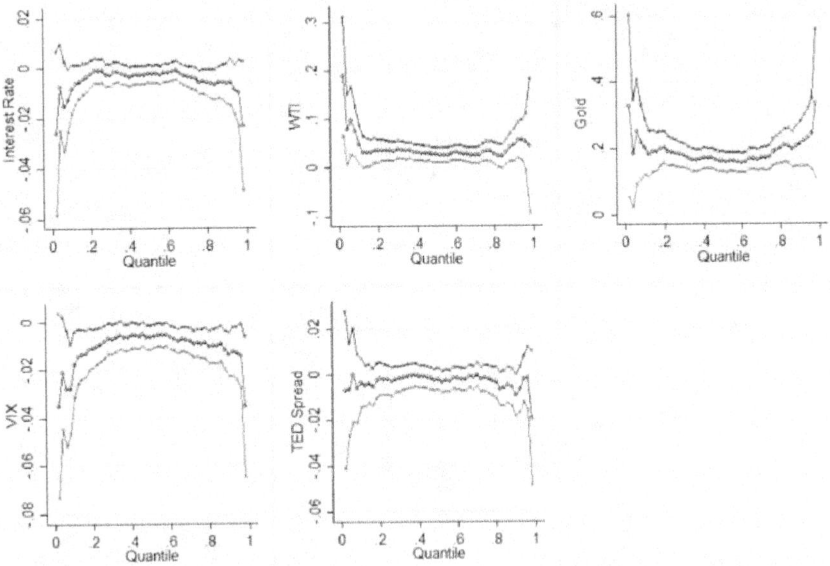

(d) EM_Asia_UQR_Economic Factors

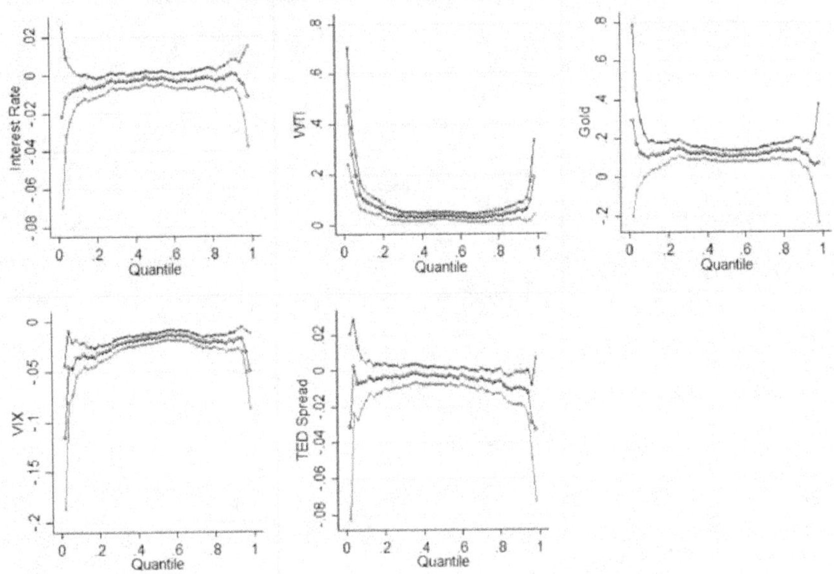

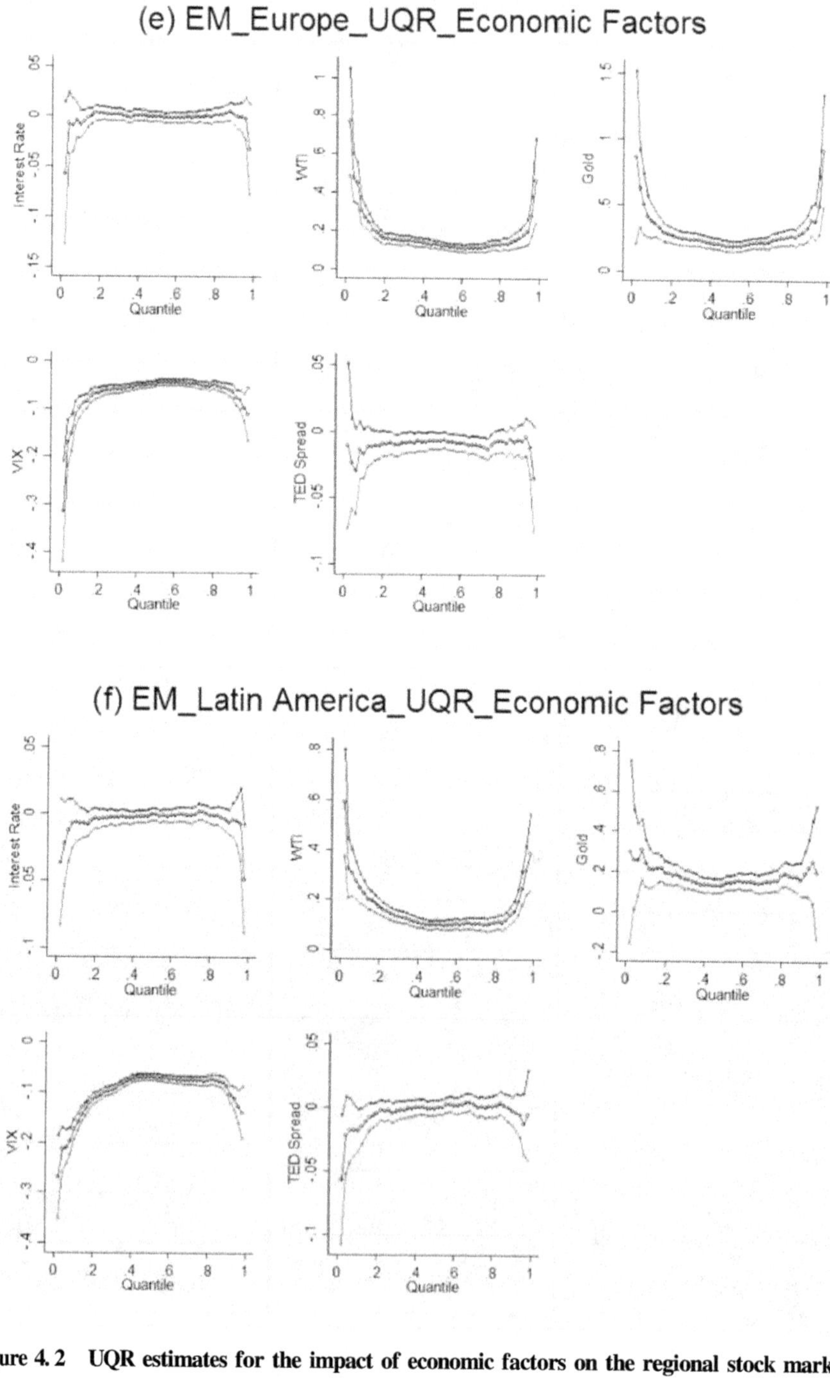

Figure 4.2 UQR estimates for the impact of economic factors on the regional stock markets

display an asymmetric n-shaped structure, except for the Developed Europe stock market, indicating that these stock markets are sensitive to changes in the IR. Moreover, the impact of a change in the IR on stock markets is more pronounced during bear markets than bull markets. The dependence structure between the stock markets and IR tends to be negative in the lower and upper quantiles; thus, IR rises (falls) lead to decreases (increases) in global stock market returns.

Regarding the two commodity markets, we observe that the dependence structures between the regional stock and oil markets show an asymmetric u-shaped structure, while the dependence structures between the regional stock and gold markets do not show the same structure. Generally, oil prices are a synchronous macroeconomic indicator of early economic expansion, and positive innovation in the global business cycle will simultaneously stimulate increases in both oil and stock prices (Chen and Lv, 2015). These asymmetric u-shaped dependence structures indicate that stock and oil prices often simultaneously rise and fall under extreme market conditions and that lower-tail dependence is much higher than upper-tail dependence. On the contrary, the effects of gold prices on regional stock markets exhibit a different pattern, perhaps because of the different features of and investors in each regional stock market. The relationships between the U. S. and Developed Europe stock and gold markets show a significant downward trend in the extreme negative stock return quantiles, implying that the safe haven property of gold for mature stock markets is more obvious.

Concerning the risk and liquidity of financial markets, the dependence structures of both the VIX and the TED spread are asymmetric n-shaped for the regional stock markets, which proves that investor sentiment has a greater effect on financial asset price in bear markets than in bull markets (Yang and Li, 2013, 2014). The asymmetric effect of the VIX indicates that bear (bull) markets are often accompanied by higher (lower) stock market risk. A stock market crash makes the market full of pessimism and anxiety, thereby affecting investors' rational decisions because of their herding behaviour, which then leads to large volatility in the financial market. Moreover, the asymmetric effect of the TED spread indicates that bear (bull) markets are often accompanied by tighter (looser) financial market liquidity. Under the "flight-to-quality" effect, fearful investors seek to sell assets perceived as risky and instead purchase safer assets (e. g. gold and U. S. Treasuries) during market turmoil, which increases liquidity pressure in the financial market. Moreover, deteriorating financial market liquidity conditions could further exacerbate stock price declines.

By using the economic factors as the explanatory variable, Tables 4. 4 and 4. 5 report the detailed UQR results for developed and emerging stock markets, respectively. Many of the coefficients of the IR are negative and significant for the U. S. stock market, while most are insignificant for the other regional stock markets, indicating that the U. S. domestic market has been more strongly influenced by changes to U. S. monetary policy than the other regional markets. Moreover, the coefficients of oil prices are positive and significant for all the regional stock markets, implying that oil is not a safe haven and hedge asset against stock markets. By contrast, the coefficients of gold prices do not show the same results. In the extreme negative stock return quantiles, we find that the coefficients of gold prices are insignificant, except for the Emerging Europe stock market, implying that gold is a safe haven asset against stock markets. This finding is consistent with that of Baur and Lucey (2010), who were the first to explicitly examine the role of gold as a safe haven. Additionally, many of the coefficients of the TED spread are negative and significant for the U. S. and Developed Europe stock markets, while many of the coefficients of the TED spread are insignificant for the other regional stock markets, indicating that market liquidity conditions have a greater impact on mature markets than on emerging markets, which is consistent with the work of Chudik and Fratzscher (2011). However, the coefficients of the VIX are negative and significant for all the regional stock markets, indicating that changes in stock market risk have a greater influence on global stock markets than changes in financial market liquidity conditions.

Table 4. 4 UQR results for the developed stock markets, using economic factors as the explanatory variable

	Q(0. 01)	Q(0. 05)	Q(0. 10)	Q(0. 50)	Q(0. 90)	Q(0. 95)	Q(0. 99)
				USA			
IR	-0. 061	-0. 016 **	-0. 011 **	0. 002 *	-0. 003	-0. 011 *	-0. 095 *
WTI	0. 540 ***	0. 132 ***	0. 054 **	0. 010 **	0. 052 ***	0. 0916 ***	0. 473 **
Gold	-0. 531	-0. 056	-0. 017	0. 007	0. 003	-0. 041	-0. 243
VIX	-0. 479 ***	-0. 229 ***	-0. 184 ***	-0. 055 ***	-0. 109 ***	-0. 121 ***	-0. 364 ***
TED	-0. 028	-0. 020 ***	-0. 015 ***	-0. 001	-0. 011 ***	-0. 017 ***	-0. 067
Cons.	-3. 431 ***	-1. 661 ***	-1. 125 ***	0. 040 ***	1. 131 ***	1. 583 ***	3. 123 ***
				Europe			
IR	-0. 000	-0. 007	-0. 005	-0. 002	0. 000	0. 000	-0. 019
WTI	1. 154 ***	0. 417 ***	0. 193 ***	0. 040 ***	0. 100 ***	0. 156 ***	0. 391 ***
Gold	-0. 041	0. 179 *	0. 193 ***	0. 140 ***	0. 176 ***	0. 251 ***	0. 236
VIX	-0. 337 ***	-0. 173 ***	-0. 111 ***	-0. 045 ***	-0. 065 ***	-0. 077 ***	-0. 100 ***
TED	-0. 029	-0. 015	-0. 021 ***	-0. 005 **	-0. 100 **	-0. 015 *	-0. 048 **
Const.	-4. 041 ***	-2. 070 ***	-1. 385 ***	0. 042 **	1. 341 ***	1. 902 ***	3. 389 ***

Continued

	Q(0. 01)	Q(0. 05)	Q(0. 10)	Q(0. 50)	Q(0. 90)	Q(0. 95)	Q(0. 99)
				Pacific			
IR	0. 030	−0. 006	−0. 008 *	−0. 002	−0. 006	−0. 007	−0. 055
WTI	0. 377 **	0. 078 **	0. 049 **	0. 027 ***	0. 047 ***	0. 048 **	0. 084
Gold	0. 503	0. 252 ***	0. 204 ***	0. 160 ***	0. 212 ***	0. 230 ***	0. 689 **
VIX	−0. 072	−0. 029 **	−0. 018 **	−0. 006 **	−0. 014 ***	−0. 012 **	−0. 040
TED	−0. 025	−0. 003	−0. 004	−0. 002	−0. 009 **	−0. 002	−0. 066
Cons.	−3. 447 ***	−1. 927 ***	−1. 275 ***	0. 048 ***	1. 332 ***	1. 747 ***	3. 183 ***

Note: ***, **, and * indicate rejection of the null hypothesis at the 1%, 5%, and 10% significance levels, respectively.

Table 4. 5 UQR results for the emerging stock markets, using economic factors as the explanatory variable

	Q(0. 01)	Q(0. 05)	Q(0. 10)	Q(0. 50)	Q(0. 90)	Q(0. 95)	Q(0. 99)
				EM_Asia			
IR	−0. 016	−0. 008	−0. 007 *	−0. 002	0. 000	−0. 004	−0. 004
WTI	0. 726 ***	0. 238 ***	0. 098 ***	0. 037 ***	0. 054 ***	0. 069 **	0. 155 **
Gold	0. 165	0. 150	0. 100 **	0. 110 ***	0. 115 ***	0. 077	0. 164
VIX	−0. 127 ***	−0. 049 ***	−0. 036 ***	−0. 017 ***	−0. 021 ***	−0. 022 ***	−0. 027
TED	−0. 043	−0. 005	−0. 006	−0. 003	−0. 010 **	−0. 020 ***	−0. 026
Cons.	−3. 933 ***	−1. 996 ***	−1. 287 ***	0. 081 ***	1. 381 ***	1. 806 ***	3. 314 ***
				EM_Europe			
IR	−0. 054	−0. 010	−0. 008	−0. 000	0. 002	−0. 001	−0. 090 *
WTI	0. 835 ***	0. 466 ***	0. 269 ***	0. 121 ***	0. 161 ***	0. 225 ***	0. 736 ***
Gold	0. 735 *	0. 563 ***	0. 380 ***	0. 185 ***	0. 326 ***	0. 442 ***	1. 002 **
VIX	−0. 265 ***	−0. 155 ***	−0. 097 ***	−0. 048 ***	−0. 063 ***	−0. 089 ***	−0. 130 **
TED	−0. 008	−0. 030 *	−0. 017 *	−0. 007 **	−0. 006	−0. 007	−0. 061
Cons.	−5. 491 ***	−2. 831 ***	−1. 850 ***	0. 088 ***	1. 824 ***	2. 513 ***	4. 713 ***

Continued

	Q(0.01)	Q(0.05)	Q(0.10)	Q(0.50)	Q(0.90)	Q(0.95)	Q(0.99)
				EM_LA			
IR	-0.079	-0.021	-0.010	-0.001	-0.006	-0.008	-0.070
WTI	0.977 ***	0.311 ***	0.244 ***	0.100 ***	0.155 ***	0.266 ***	0.636 ***
Gold	0.211	0.307 ***	0.239 ***	0.134 ***	0.161 ***	0.254 ***	0.076
VIX	-0.408 ***	-0.215 ***	-0.175 ***	-0.070 ***	-0.088 ***	-0.113 ***	-0.222 ***
TED	-0.073	-0.019	-0.018 **	-0.000	-0.002	-0.009	-0.034
Cons.	-5.104 ***	-2.684 ***	-1.814 ***	0.077 ***	1.757 ***	2.426 ***	4.291 ***

Note: ***, **, and * indicate rejection of the null hypothesis at the 1%, 5%, and 10% significance levels, respectively.

4.4.3 Comparison of the UQR and CQR Results

The CQR approach shows the effect of a covariate on the different quantiles of the outcome variable conditional on specific covariates (x); thus, the size, significance, and direction of the effect can change according to the specification. However, the UQR approach can address the above shortcoming because it allows us to analyse the outcome variable over its entire distribution. Figure 4.3 presents the CQR estimates for the U.S. and Developed Europe stock markets.① We observe large differences in the results compared with Figure 4.1. The relationships among many of the regional stock markets show asymmetric u-shaped structures in Figure 4.1, whereas this structure is not obvious in Figure 4.3. In particular, the U.S. market displays an asymmetric

① To save space, the results for the other regional stock markets are not reported and are available on request.

N-shaped dependence structure for the Developed Europe market in Figure 4. 1, while Figure 4. 3 provides a result in the opposite direction. Similarly, the results of Figure 4. 2 show that the impacts of the economic factors on the regional stock markets are mostly significant and asymmetric u-shaped or n-shaped dependence structures; in other words, the economic factors have a greater impact on the lower quantiles than on the upper quantiles. However, the structure that the lower quantiles are more strongly influenced by the economic factors is difficult to obtain in Figure 4. 3. These findings indicate that we obtain different results when applying the entire distributions of the outcome variable and the distributions of the outcome variable based on specific covariates.

(a) USA_CQR_Stock Markets

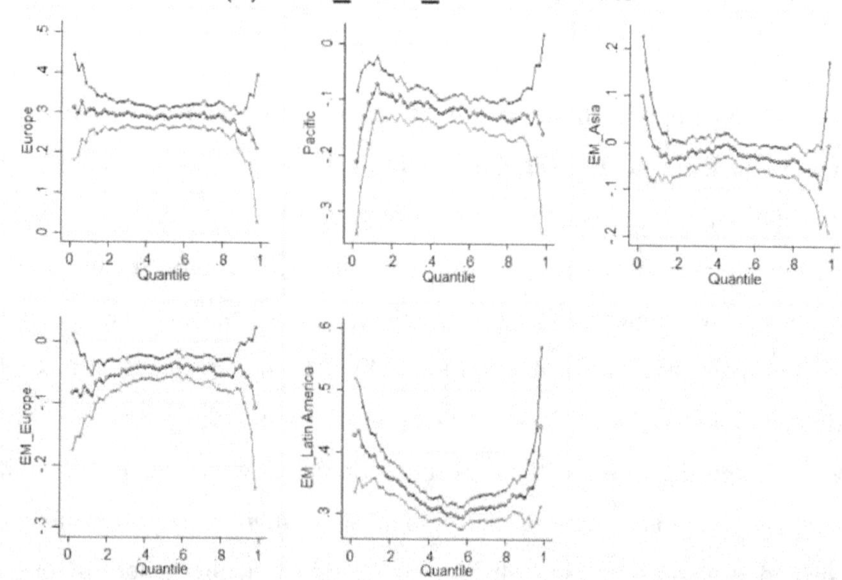

(b) Europe_CQR_Stock Markets

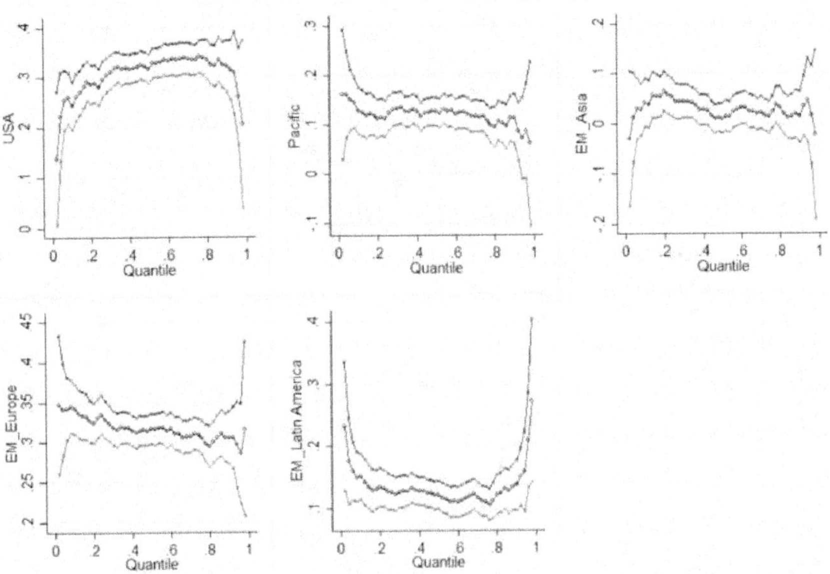

(c) USA_CQR_Economic Factors

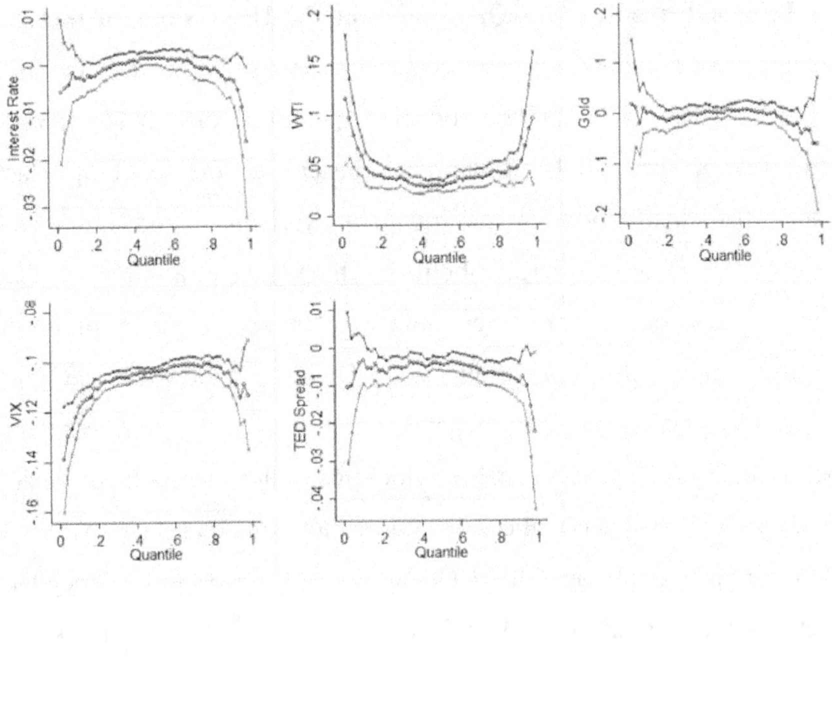

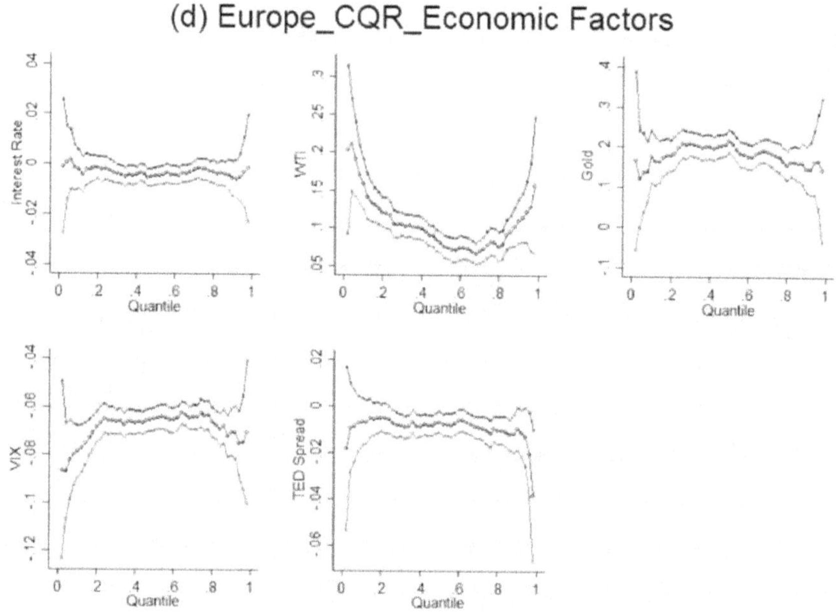

Figure 4. 3 CQR estimates for the U. S. and Developed Europe stock markets

Table 4. 6 reports the CQR results for the U. S. stock market. We find that the dependence structures for extreme market conditions (in the 1%, 5%, 10%, 90%, 95%, and 99% quantiles) display larger values when we consider the UQR approach instead of the CQR approach. Hence, the distribution of the outcome variable based on specific covariates is an incomplete distribution, which leads to a failure to obtain accurate dependence structures under extreme market conditions. Moreover, unlike the UQR results, the CQR results show that the IR and TED spread have insignificant dependence structures for extreme negative stock returns in the U. S. market, which lose a lot of useful information in capturing the impact of the economic factors on stock markets.

Overall, we introduce the UQR approach to explore the dependence structures for the different quantiles of the regional stock markets to obtain more accurate extreme-value relationships and more significant asymmetric effects. We conclude that the results obtained from the UQR approach provide more useful information for investors and policymakers.

Table 4. 6 CQR results for the U. S. stock market

	Q(0. 01)	Q(0. 05)	Q(0. 10)	Q(0. 50)	Q(0. 90)	Q(0. 95)	Q(0. 99)
	Using the other regional stock markets as explanatory variable.						
Europe	0. 311 *	0. 309 ***	0. 307 ***	0. 291 ***	0. 248 ***	0. 260 ***	0. 210
Pacific	−0. 197	−0. 127 **	−0. 089 ***	−0. 117 ***	−0. 128 ***	−0. 147 ***	−0. 251
EM_Asia	0. 201	0. 027	−0. 013	−0. 016	−0. 067 **	−0. 087 *	0. 094
EM_Europe	−0. 134	−0. 078 **	−0. 082 ***	−0. 042 ***	−0. 039 **	−0. 061 *	−0. 124
EM_LA	0. 391 ***	0. 420 ***	0. 391 ***	0. 298 ***	0. 325 ***	0. 350 ***	0. 408 **
Cons.	−2. 204 ***	−1. 233 ***	−0. 827 ***	0. 026 ***	0. 814 ***	1. 187 ***	2. 148 ***
	Using the economic factors as explanatory variable.						
IR	−0. 008	−0. 005	−0. 003	0. 001 *	−0. 003	−0. 007 *	−0. 022
WTI	0. 103	0. 089 ***	0. 060 ***	0. 030 ***	0. 048 ***	0. 076 ***	0. 098
Gold	0. 006	−0. 020	0. 000	0. 001	−0. 042 **	−0. 071 **	−0. 008
VIX	−0. 148 ***	−0. 130 ***	−0. 118 ***	−0. 104 ***	−0. 108 ***	−0. 112 ***	−0. 107 ***
TED	−0. 012	−0. 008	−0. 003	−0. 004 ***	−0. 010 ***	−0. 014 **	−0. 023
Const.	−2. 110 ***	−1. 016 ***	−0. 653 ***	0. 004	0. 709 ***	1. 067 ***	2. 176 ***

Note: ***, **, and * indicate rejection of the null hypothesis at the 1%, 5%, and 10% significance levels, respectively.

4. 5 Conclusions

In this study, we assess the dependence structures for the different quantiles of six regional stock markets. Specifically, we not only examine the dependence structures among these regional stock markets, but also explore the asymmetric effects of economic factors on them. To this end, we apply the UQR approach instead of the traditional CQR approach, as it can avoid the effect of the distributions of specific covariates on the results. Moreover, we also compare the results obtained from the UQR and CQR approaches.

By using daily data for 2 January 2003 to 30 March 2018, our empirical results indicate that there are great differences between the structure and degree of dependence obtained from the UQR and CQR approaches and that the UQR approach can provide more accurate extreme-value relationships and more significant asymmetric effects than the CQR approach. Regarding the dependence structures among the six regional stock markets, we find that most show asymmetric u-shaped structures, indicating that the contagion effect among stock markets becomes stronger under extreme market conditions, especially in bear markets. More importantly, geographically and economically close regional stock markets exhibit significant influences over each other, which provides useful information for international investors because of the strengthening of transnational investment.

Concerning the asymmetric effects of the economic factors on the six regional stock markets, we find that the IR displays an asymmetric n-shaped structure, implying that IR rises (falls) lead to decreases (increases) in stock market returns. Moreover, oil markets show an asymmetric u-shaped structure for stock markets, indicating that large downward (upward) oil prices lead to large downward (upward) stock prices, especially in the lower quantiles. By contrast, the coefficients of gold prices are insignificant in the lower quantiles, implying that gold has a weak safe haven property against stock markets. As for the risk and liquidity in financial markets, both the VIX and the TED spread show asymmetric n-shaped structures. This result suggests that bear (bull) markets are often accompanied by higher (lower) stock market risk and larger (smaller) financial market liquidity pressure. Additionally, the IR has a greater impact on the U. S. market and the TED spread has a greater impact on the U. S. and Developed Europe markets, implying that mature markets are more strongly impacted by these economic factors than emerging markets.

Our analysis provides some policy implications for policymakers and international investors. First, the empirical results provide evidence of a heterogeneous dependence structure for the different quantiles of these six regional stock markets. Owing to herding behaviour, investors' fear (greed) is magnified in bear (bull) markets, thereby affecting their rational decisions, which then leads to frenzied selling (buying) and crashes (bubble). These findings indicate that the structure and degree of dependence vary in the different quantiles of stock markets. Thus, governments (investors) should frequently adjust their policies (portfolios) according to the varying market conditions. Second, the distance between markets and market characteristics are the primary determinants of the relationships among stock markets. Investors could add geographically and economically alienated stock market assets to their traditional portfolios to reduce investment risk. Third, with the financialization of commodity markets, both oil and gold exert a significant influence on stock markets. Oil and stock prices show a high degree of synchronicity under the same economic fundamentals. As such, investors can predict rises and falls in stock prices based on oil market conditions, which can help them reduce the cost of forecasting stock prices. By contrast, since gold has a safe haven property, investors can invest more heavily in the gold asset in their portfolios to reduce overall losses when markets are stressed. Finally, different monetary regimes and financial market liquidity conditions have asymmetric effects on stock prices. The U. S. government should thus adopt a loose monetary policy (low interest rate) and ensure adequate financial market liquidity (a low TED spread) to stimulate stock market growth when the global stock market is at a low point, and this approach is more effective for mature markets.

Chapter 5

Conclusions

This thesis is constituted by three essays that explore the global stock market nexus considering external factors. We divide global external factors into two major categories: other stock markets and global economic factors. Due to the globalization and integration of financial markets, this thesis not only examines the relationships among stock markets, but also explores the impact of global economic factors on them. Chapter 2 and Chapter 3 investigate the emerging Asian stock markets because of their marketization and large amount of FDI outflows, and in Chapter 4, we examine the global regional stock markets given the regional financial integration.

In Chapter 2, we answer the question of what global economic factors drive emerging Asian stock market returns. We find that financial variables show a stronger relationship with emerging Asian stock markets in-sample, while economic fundamentals have stronger predictive power for emerging Asian stock markets out-of-sample. Additionally, the role of global factors was significantly stronger during regional and global financial crises.

In Chapter 3, we evaluate the influence of exogenous shocks on time-varying relationships and portfolio strategies between the emerging Asian and other global stock markets. We find that if we consider exogenous shocks in our models, we will obtain more accurate results and better hedging strategies. Moreover, results show significant variability in the relationships between all two pairs of stock markets, and developed stock asset is a cheaper hedge asset than other global emerging stock asset.

In Chapter 4, we assess the asymmetric dependence structures for global regional stock markets according to different market conditions. We find convincing evidence that contagion effect among stock markets becomes stronger under extreme market conditions. Moreover, impacts of global economic factors on stock markets are more pronounced during bear and bull markets than during normal markets, especially so in bear markets.

The findings of this thesis have several important implications for policymakers, academic researchers, and international investors. Both the relationships among and the effect of global economic factors on stock markets can change with time and market conditions. Thus, governments (investors) should frequently adjust their policies (portfolios) according to the varying market situations. The results of relationships among stock markets indicate that market characteristics and distance between markets are their primary determinants. International investors could incorporate economically and geographically alienated stock market assets in their traditional portfolios to reduce investment risk.

There are a wide range of global economic factors that can affect stock returns, where the impacts of these global factors become stronger under extreme market conditions. Hence, stock markets need to build an effective market mechanism for hedging against the risks imposed by global markets. Moreover, researchers should pay greater attention to the impact of exogenous shocks on stock markets when they analyse economic issues. It is worth mentioning that this thesis considers a large number of global economic factors, these factors represent significant global economic information and monetary policy decisions. More importantly, these global factors can play their respective roles in the stock market under different market conditions. Take USD and gold as examples, investors could consider constructing diversified portfolios including such assets, because these two assets can show a negative or insignificant relationship with stock returns during regular and extreme market periods, respectively.

Appendices

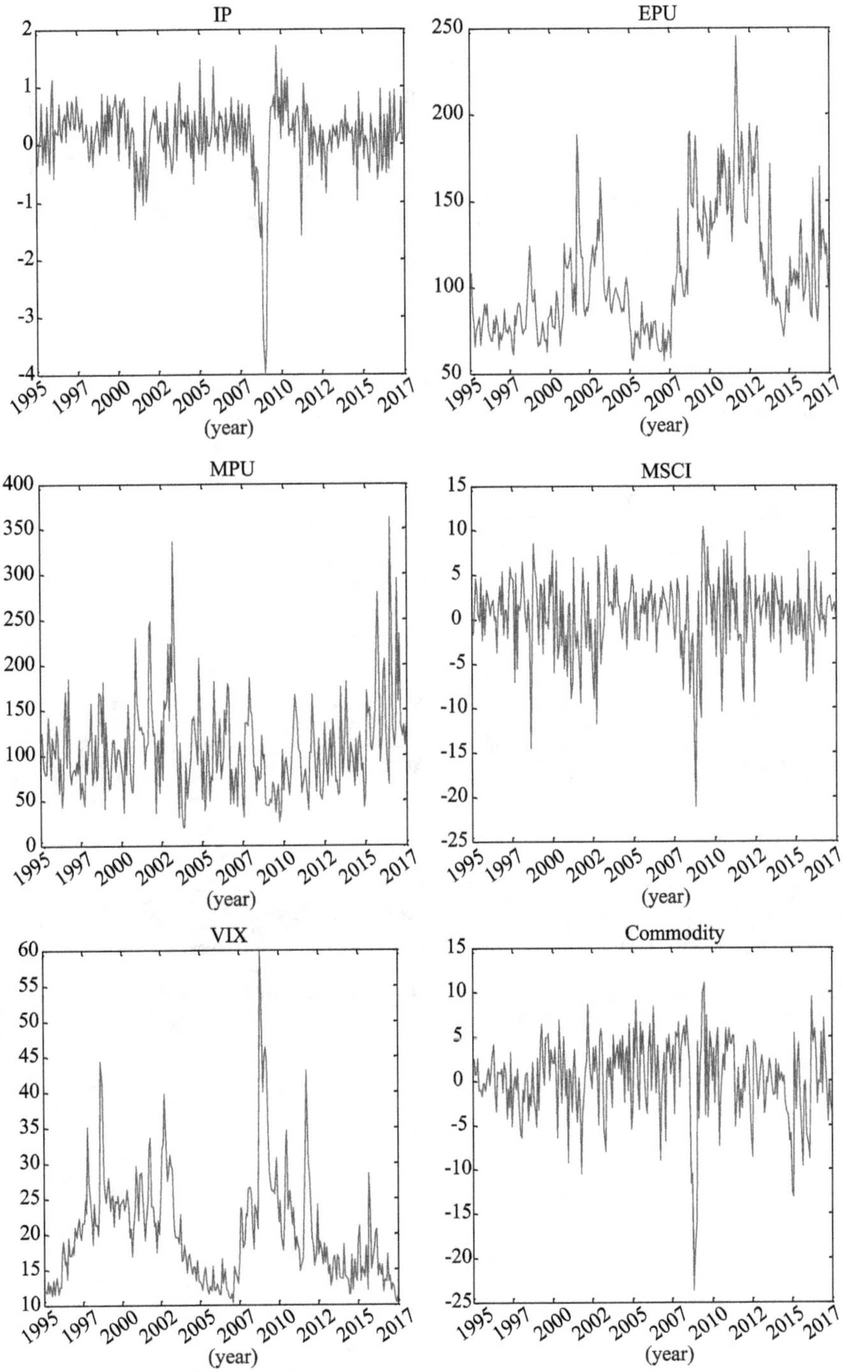
IP
2
1
0
-1
-2
-3
-4
1995 1997 2000 2002 2005 2007 2010 2012 2015 2017
(year)
EPU
250
200
150
100
50
1995 1997 2000 2002 2005 2007 2010 2012 2015 2017
(year)
MPU
400
350
300
250
200
150
100
50
0
1995 1997 2000 2002 2005 2007 2010 2012 2015 2017
(year)
MSCI
15
10
5
0
-5
-10
-15
-20
-25
1995 1997 2000 2002 2005 2007 2010 2012 2015 2017
(year)
VIX
60
55
50
45
40
35
30
25
20
15
10
1995 1997 2000 2002 2005 2007 2010 2012 2015 2017
(year)
Commodity
15
10
5
0
-5
-10
-15
-20
-25
1995 1997 2000 2002 2005 2007 2010 2012 2015 2017
(year)

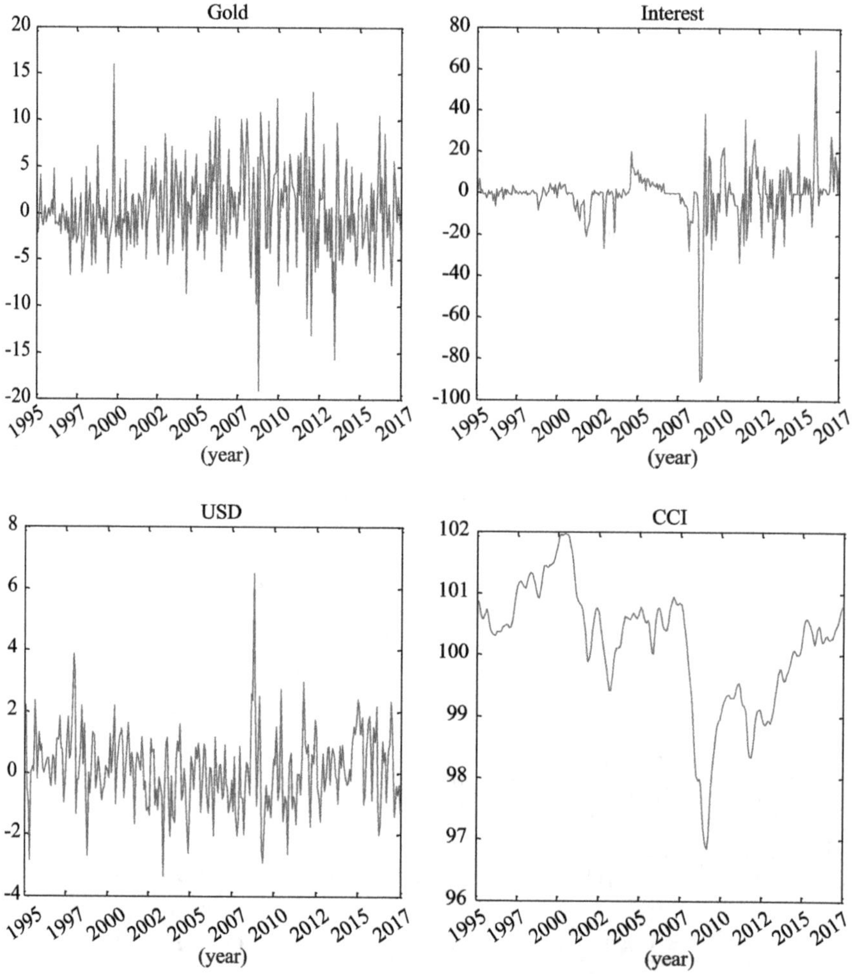

Appendix Figure 2. 1 10 potential global economic factors

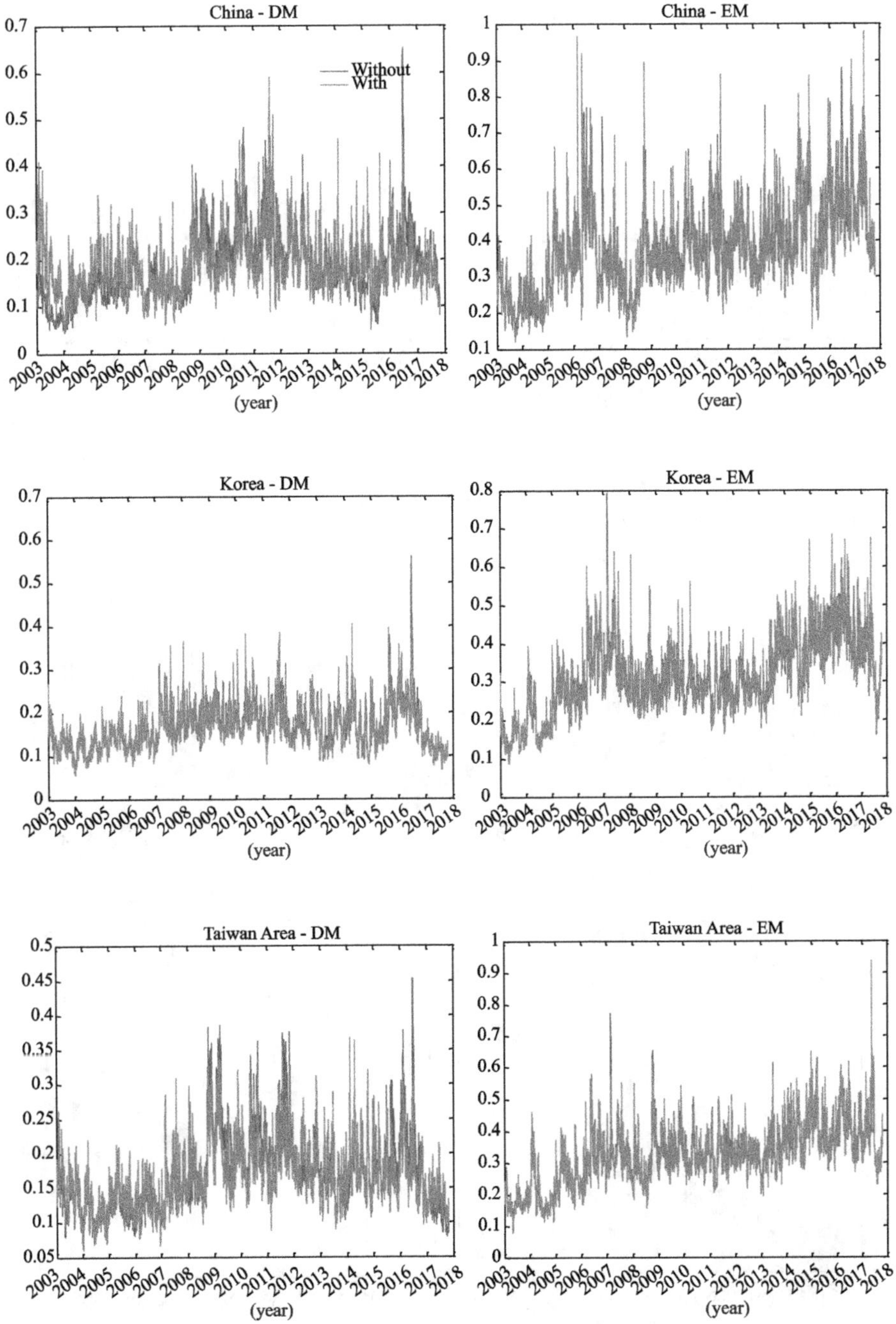
China - DM
Without
With
China - EM
Korea - DM
Korea - EM
Taiwan Area - DM
Taiwan Area - EM
(year)
2003
2004
2005
2006
2007
2008
2009
2010
2011
2012
2013
2014
2015
2016
2017
2018

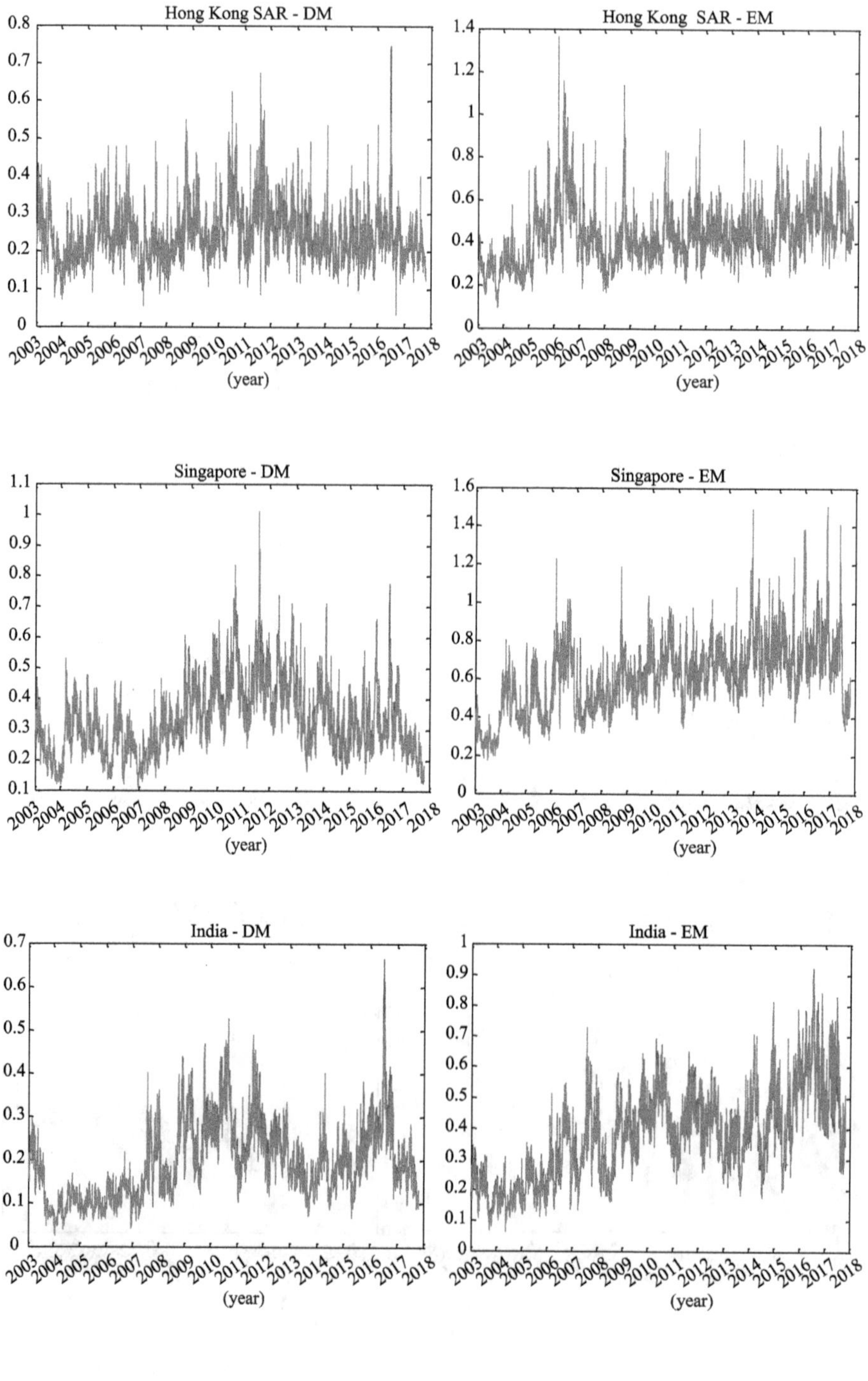
Hong Kong SAR - DM
Hong Kong SAR - EM
Singapore - DM
Singapore - EM
India - DM
India - EM
(year)

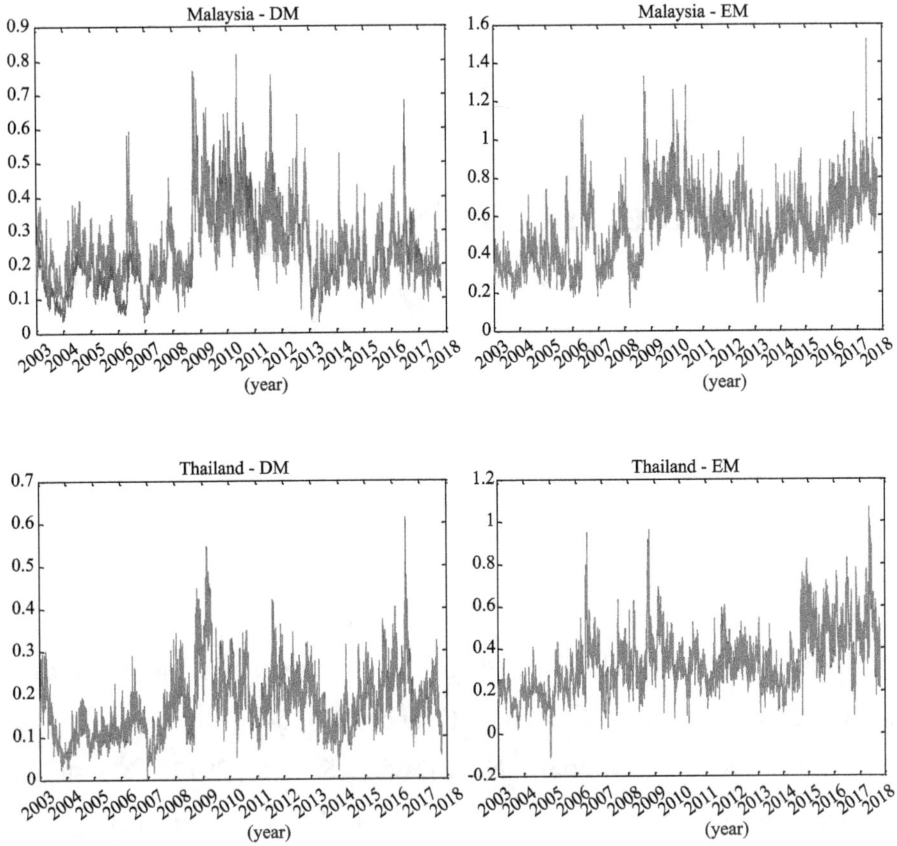

Appendix Figure 3. 1 Time-varying hedging ratios, with and without exogenous shocks

References (by Chapter)

Chapter 1

Baker, M., Wurgler, J., 2006. Investor sentiment and the cross-section of stock returns. Journal of Finance 61, 1645—1680.

Baker, S. R., Bloom, N., Davis, S. J., 2012. Measuring economic policy uncertainty. Working Paper, Stanford University.

Balli, F., Hajhoj, H. R., Basherd, S. A., Ghassan, H. B., 2015. An analysis of returns and volatility spillovers and their determinants in emerging Asian and Middle Eastern countries. International Review of Economics and Finance 39, 311—325.

Baur, D. G., Lucey, B., 2010. Is gold a hedge or safe haven? An analysis of stocks bonds and gold. Financial Review 45 (2), 217—229.

Beaudry, P., Koop, G., 1993. Do recessions permanently change output? Journal of Monetary Economics 31 (2), 149—163.

Bollerslev, T., Chou, R. Y., Kroner, K. F., 1992. ARCH modeling in finance: A review of the theory and empirical evidence.

Journal of Econometrics, 52 (1—2), 5—59.

Branson, W. H., 1983. Macroeconomic determinants of real exchange risk. In: Herring, R. J. (Ed.), Managing Foreign Exchange Rate Risk. Cambridge University Press, Cambridge, 33—74.

Brock, W. A., Hommes, C. H., 1998. Heterogeneous beliefs and routes to chaos in a simple asset pricing model. Journal of Economic Dynamics and Control, 22, 1235—1274.

Chen, Q., Lv, X., 2015. The extreme-value dependence between the crude oil price and Chinese stock markets. International Review of Economics and Finance 39, 121—132.

Chien, M.-S., Lee, C.-C., Hu, T.-C., Hu, H,-T, 2015. Dynamic Asian stock market convergence: Evidence from dynamic cointegration analysis among China and ASEAN-5. Economic Modelling 51, 84—98.

Chudik, A., Fratzscher, M., 2011. Identifying the global transmission of the 2007—2009 financial crisis in a GVAR model. European Economic Review 55, 325—339.

Day, R. H., 1983. The emergence of chaos from classical economic growth. The Quarterly Journal of Economics 98 (2), 201—213.

Day, R. H., 1992. Complex economic dynamics: obvious in history, generic in theory, elusive in data. Journal of Applied Econometrics 7, S9—S23.

Entorf, H., Gross, A., Steiner, C., 2012. Business cycle forecasts and their implications for high frequency stock market returns. Journal of Forecasting 31, 1—14.

Fama, E. F., 1970. Efficient capital markets: a review of theory and empirical work. Journal of Finance 25 (2), 383—417.

Fama, E. F., 1998. Market efficiency, long-term returns, and behavioral finance. Journal of Financial Economics 49 (3), 283—306.

Fama, E. F., French, K. R., 1992. The cross-section of expected stock returns. Journal of Finance 47, 427—465.

Fama, E. F., French, K. R., 2015. A five-factor asset pricing model. Journal of Financial Economics 116 (1), 1—22.

Firpo, S., Fortin, N. M., Lemieux, T., 2009. Unconditional quantile regression. Econometrica 77 (3), 953—973.

Guesmi, K., Nguyen, D. K., 2011. How strong is the global integration of emerging market regions? An empirical assessment. Economic Modelling 28, 2517—2527.

Husted, L., Rogers, J. H., Sun, B., 2017. Monetary policy uncertainty. Working Paper, Board of Governors of the Federal Reserve Board.

Kelsey, D., 1988. The economics of chaos or the chaos of economics. Oxford Economic Papers New Series 40 (1), 1—31.

Kenourgios, D., Dimitriou, D., 2015. Contagion of the Global Financial Crisis and the real economy: a regional analysis. Economic Modelling 44, 283—293.

Kenourgios, D., Padhi, P., 2012. Emerging markets and financial crises: Regional, global or isolated shocks? Journal of Multinational Financial Management 22, 24—38.

Koop, G., Korobilis, D., 2012. Forecasting inflation using dynamic model averaging. International Economic Review 53, 867—886.

Laopodis, N. T., 2013. Monetary policy and stock market dynamics across monetary regimes. Journal of International Money and Finance 33, 381—406.

Li, Y. , Giles, D. E. , 2015. Modelling volatility spillover effects between developed stock markets and Asian emerging stock markets. International Journal of Finance & Economics 20, 155—177.

Lorenz, E. , 1963. Deterministic nonperiodic flow. Journal of Atmospheric Science 20, 130—141.

Markowitz, H. , 1952. Portfolio selection. Journal of Finance 7 (1), 77—91.

Mensi, W. , Hammoudeh, S. , Kang, S. H. , 2017. Risk spillovers and portfolio management between developed and BRICS stock markets. North American Journal of Economics and Finance 41, 133—155.

Nasser, O. M. A. , Hajilee, M. , 2016. Integration of emerging stock markets with global stock markets. Research in International Business and Finance 36, 1—12.

Prabheesh, K. P. , Vidya, C. T. , 2018. Do business cycles, investment-specific technology shocks matter for stock returns? Economic Modelling 70, 511—524.

Shiller, R. J. , 2015. Irrational exuberance. Princeton University Press, Princeton, New Jersey.

Shintani, N. , Linton, O. , 2004. Non parametric neutral network estimation of Lyapunov exponent and a direct test for chaos. Journal of Econometrics 120, 1—33.

Chapter 2

Aloui, C. , Hammoudeh, S. , Hamida, H. B. , 2015. Global factors driving structural changes in the co-movement between sharia stocks and sukuk in the Gulf Cooperation Council countries. North American Journal of Economics and Finance 31, 311—329.

Aye, G. C., Gupta, R., Hammoudeh, S., Kim, W. J., 2015. Forecasting the price of gold using dynamic model averaging. International Review of Financial Analysis 41, 257—266.

Baker, M., Wurgler, J., 2006. Investor sentiment and the cross-section of stock returns. Journal of Finance 61, 1645—1680.

Baker, S. R., Bloom, N., Davis, S. J., 2012. Measuring economic policy uncertainty. Working Paper, Stanford University.

Balcilar, M., Demirer, R., Hammoudeh, S., 2014. What drives herding in oil-rich, developing stock markets? Relative roles of own volatility and global factors. North American Journal of Economics and Finance 29, 418—440.

Barberis, N., Shleifer, A., Vishny, R., 1998. A model of investor sentiment. Journal of Financial Economics 49 (3), 307—343.

Baur, D. G., Beckmann, J., Czudaj, R., 2016. A melting pot – gold price forecasts under model and parameter uncertainty. International Review of Financial Analysis 48, 282—291.

Bork, L., Moller, S. V., 2015. Forecasting house prices in the 50 states using dynamic model averaging and dynamic model selection. International Journal of Forecasting 31, 63—78.

Branson, W. H., 1983. Macroeconomic determinants of real exchange risk. In: Herring, R. J. (Ed.), Managing Foreign Exchange Rate Risk. Cambridge University Press, Cambridge, 33—74.

Cogley, T., Sargent, T., 2005. Drifts and volatilities: monetary policies and outcomes in the post WWII U. S.. Review of Economic Dynamics 8, 262—302.

Davis, S. J., 2016. An index of global economic policy

uncertainty. NBER Working Paper No. 22740, National Bureau of Economic Research.

Drachal, K., 2016. Forecasting spot oil price in a dynamic model averaging framework—have the determinants changed over time? Energy Economics 60, 35—46.

Entorf, H., Gross, A., Steiner, C., 2012. Business cycle forecasts and their implications for high frequency stock market returns. Journal of Forecasting 31, 1—14.

Fama, E. F., 1970. Efficient capital markets: a review of theory and empirical work. Journal of Finance 25 (2), 383—417.

Fama, E. F., 1998. Market efficiency, long-term returns, and behavioral finance. Journal of Financial Economics 49 (3), 283—306.

Filippo, G. D., 2015. Dynamic model averaging and CPI inflation forecasts: a comparison between the euro area and the United States. Journal of Forecasting 34, 619—648.

Frankel, J. A., 1983. Monetary and portfolio-balance models of exchange rate determination. In: Bhandari, J. S., Putnam, B. H., Levin, J. H. (Eds.), Economic Interdependence and Flexible Exchange Rates. MIT Press, Cambridge, 84—115.

Füss, R., 2005. Financial liberalization and stock price behaviour in Asian emerging markets. Economic Change and Restructuring 38 (1), 37—62.

Geweke, J., Amisano, G., 2011. Hierarchical Markov normal mixture models with applications to financial asset returns. Journal of Applied Econometrics 26, 1—29.

Gupta, R., Hammoudeh, S., Kim, W. J., Simo-Kengne, B. D., 2014. Forecasting China's foreign exchange reserves using dynamic model averaging: the role of macroeconomic fundamentals, financial stress and economic uncertainty. North American Journal of Economics and Finance 28, 170—189.

Hammoudeh, S., Sari, R., Uzunkaya, M., Liu, T., 2013. The dynamics of BRICS's country risk ratings and domestic stock markets, U. S. stock market and oil price. Mathematics and Computers in Simulation 94, 277—294.

Hoeting, J. A., Madigan, D., Raftery, A. E., Volinsky, C. T., 1999. Bayesian model averaging: a tutorial. Statistical Science 14, 382—417.

Husted, L., Rogers, J. H., Sun, B., 2017. Monetary policy uncertainty. Working Paper, Board of Governors of the Federal Reserve Board.

Hwang, E., Min, H. G., Kim, B.-H., Kim, H., 2013. Determinants of stock market comovements among US and emerging economies during the US financial crisis. Economic Modelling 35, 338—348.

Jouini, J., 2013. Stock markets in GCC countries and global factors: a further investigation. Economic Modelling 31, 80—86.

Kim, B.-H., Kim, H., Lee, B.-S., 2015. Spillover effects of the U. S. financial crisis on financial markets in emerging Asian countries. International Review of Economics and Finance 39, 192—210.

Koop, G., Korobilis, D., 2011. UK macroeconomic forecasting with many predictors: which models forecast best and when do they do so? Economic Modelling 28 (5), 2307—2318.

Koop, G., Korobilis, D., 2012. Forecasting inflation using dynamic model averaging. International Economic Review 53, 867—886.

Liang, C. -C., Lin, J. -B., Hsu, H. -C., 2013. Reexamining the relationships between stock prices and exchange rates in ASEAN—5 using panel Granger causality approach. Economic Modelling 32, 560—563.

Li, Y., Giles, D. E., 2015. Modelling volatility spillover effects between developed stock markets and Asian emerging stock markets. International Journal of Finance & Economics 20, 155—177.

Marr, J., Reynard, C., 2010. Investing in emerging markets: the BRIC economies and beyond. Wiley Online Library.

Mensi, W., Hammoudeh, S., Reboredo, J. C., Nguyen, D. K., 2014. Do global factors impact BRICS stock markets? A quantile regression approach. Emerging Markets Review 19, 1—17.

Mensi, W., Hammoudeh, S., Yoon, S. -M., Balcilar, M., 2017. Impact of macroeconomic factors and country risk ratings on GCC stock markets: evidence from a dynamic panel threshold model with regime switching. Applied Economics 49 (13), 1255—1272.

Mollah, S., Quoreshi, A. M. M. S., Zafirov, G., 2016. Equity market contagion during global financial and eurozone crises: evidence from a dynamic correlation analysis. Journal of International Financial Markets, Institutions & Money 41, 151—167.

Naser, H., 2016. Estimating and forecasting the real prices of crude oil: a data rich model using a dynamic model averaging (DMA) approach. Energy Economics 56, 75—87.

Naser, R., Skjeltorp, J. A., Ødegaard, B. A., 2011. Stock market liquidity and the business cycle. Journal of Finance 66 (1), 139—176.

Nasser, O. M. A., Hajilee, M., 2016. Integration of emerging stock markets with global stock markets. Research in International

Business and Finance 36, 1—12.

Prabheesh, K. P., Vidya, C. T., 2018. Do business cycles, investment-specific technology shocks matter for stock returns? Economic Modelling 70, 511—524.

Primiceri, G., 2005. Time-varying structural vector autoregressions and monetary policy. Review of Economic Studies 72, 821—52.

Raftery, A. E., Kárn'y, M., Ettler, P., 2010. Online prediction under model uncertainty via dynamic model averaging: application to a cold rolling mill. Technometrics 52 (1), 52—66.

Rapach, D. E., Strauss, J. K., Zhou, G., 2013. International stock return predictability: what is the role of the United States? Journal of Finance 68 (4), 1633—1662.

Reboredo, J. C., Rivera-Castro, M. A., Ugolini, A., 2016. Downside and upside risk spillovers between exchange rates and stock prices. Journal of Banking and Finance 62, 76—96.

Richards, A., 2005. Big fish in small ponds: the trading behavior and price impact of foreign investors in Asian emerging equity markets. Journal of Financial and Quantitative Analysis 40 (1), 1—27.

Risse, M., Kern, M., 2016. Forecasting house-price growth in the euro area with dynamic model averaging. North American Journal of Economics and Finance 38, 70—85.

Shiller, R. J., 2015. Irrational Exuberance. Princeton University Press, Princeton, New Jersey.

Sugimoto, K., Matsuki, T., Yoshida, Y., 2014. The global financial crisis: an analysis of the spillover effects on African stock markets. Emerging Markets Review 21, 201—233.

Wei, Y., Cao, Y., 2017. Forecasting house prices using dynamic model averaging approach: evidence from China. Economic Modelling

61, 147—155.

Chapter 3

Aggarwal, R. , Inclán, C. , Leal. R. , 1999. Volatility in emerging stock markets. Journal of Financial and Quantitative Analysis 34 (1), 33—55.

Aielli, G. P. , 2013. Dynamic conditional correlation: on properties and estimation. Journal of Business and Economic Statistics 31, 282—299.

Aloui, C. , 2011. Latin American stock markets' volatility spillovers during the financial crises: a multivariate FIAPARCH-DCC framework. Macroeconomics and Finance in Emerging Market Economies 4 (2), 289—326.

Baillie, R. T. , Bollerslev, T. , Mikkelsen, H. O. , 1996. Fractionally integrated generalized autoregressive conditional heteroscedasticity. Journal of Econometrics 74, 3—30.

Baker, S. R. , Bloom, N. , Davis, S. J. , 2015. Measuring economic policy uncertainty. National Bureau of Economic Research, Working Paper No. w21633.

Bano, S. , Tabbada, J. , 2015. Foreign direct investment outflows: Asian developing countries. Journal of Economic Integration 30 (2), 359—398.

Bekaert, G. , Harvey, C. R. , 1995. Time-varying world market integration. Journal of Finance 50, 403—444.

Bollerslev, T. , Mikkelsen, H. O. , 1996. Modeling and pricing long-memory in stock market volatility. Journal of Econometrics 73, 151—184.

Bollerslev, T., Mikkelsen, H. O., 1999. Long-term equity anticipation securities and stock market volatility dynamics. Journal of Econometrics 92, 75—99.

Bolloverslev, T., Wright, J. H., 2001. High-frequency data, frequency domain inference, and volatility forecasting. The Review of Economics and Statistics 83, 596—602.

Cheung, Y. -L., Mak, S. -C., 1992. The international transmission of stock market fluctuations between the developed markets and the Asian—Pacific markets. Applied Financial Economics 2, 43—47.

Cotter, J., Hanly, J., 2012. Hedging effectiveness under conditions of asymmetry. European Journal of Finance 18 (2), 135—147.

Dickey, D. A., Fuller, W., 1979. Distribution of the estimators for autoregressive time series with a unit root. Journal of the American Statistical Association 74 (336), 427—431.

Dimitriou, D., Kenourgios, D., Simos, T., 2013. Global financial crisis and emerging stock market contagion: a multivariate FIAPARCH - DCC approach. International Review of Financial Analysis 30, 46—56.

Dong, X., Yoon, S. -M., 2018. Structural breaks, dynamic correlations, and hedge and safe havens for stock and foreign exchange markets in Greater China. World Economy 41 (10), 2783—2803.

Engle, R. F., 1982. Autoregressive conditional heteroskedasticity with estimates of the variance of United Kingdom inflation. Econometrica 50 (4), 987—1007.

Engle, R. F., 2002. Dynamic conditional correlation: a simple class of multivariate generalized autoregressive conditional heteroskedasticity models. Journal of Business & Economic Statistics 20,

339—350.

Geweke, J., Porter-Hudak, S., 1983. The estimation and application of long memory time series models. Journal of Time Series Analysis 4 (4), 221—238.

Hammoudeh, S., Li, H., 2008. Sudden changes in volatility in emerging markets: the case of Gulf Arab stock markets. International Review of Financial Analysis 17 (1), 47—63.

Inclán, C., Tiao, G. C., 1994. Use of cumulative sums of squares for retrospective detection of changes of variance. Journal of the American Statistical Association 89, 913—923.

Jarque, C. M., Bera, A. K., 1980. Efficient tests for normality, homoscedasticity and serial independence of regression residuals. Economic Letters 6 (3), 255—259.

Kang, S. H., Cho, H.-G., Yoon, S.-M., 2009. Modeling sudden volatility changes: evidence from Japanese and Korean stock markets. Physica A: Statistical Mechanics and its Applications 388 (17), 3543—3550.

Kang, S. H., McIver, R., Yoon, S.-M., 2016. Modeling time-varying correlations in volatility between BRICS and commodity markets. Emerging Markets Finance and Trade 52 (7), 1698—1723.

Kenourgios, D., Dimitriou, D., 2015. Contagion of the Global Financial Crisis and the real economy: a regional analysis. Economic Modelling 44, 283—293.

Kim, B.-H., Kim, H., Lee, B.-S., 2015. Spillover effects of the U.S. financial crisis on financial markets in emerging Asian countries. International Review of Economics and Finance 39, 192—210.

Kolstad, I., Wiig, A., 2012. What determines Chinese outward

FDI? Journal of World Business 47, 26—34.

Kroner, K. F., Ng, V. K., 1998. Modeling asymmetric comovements of asset returns. Review of Financial Studies 1 (4), 817—844.

Kroner, K. F., Sultan, J., 1993. Time dynamic varying distributions and dynamic hedging with foreign currency futures. Journal of Financial and Quantitative Analysis 28 (4), 535—551.

Kuester, K., Mittnik, S., Paolella, M., 2006. Value-at-risk prediction: a comparison of alternative strategies. Journal of Financial Econometrics 4, 53—89.

Kupiec, P., 1995. Techniques for verifying the accuracy of risk measurement models. Journal of Derivatives 3 (2), 17—184.

Ku, Y.-H., Chen, H.-C., Chen, K.-H., 2007. On the application of the dynamic conditional correlation model in estimating optimal time-varying hedge ratios. Applied Economics Letters 14, 503—509.

Kwiatkowski, D., Phillips, P. C. B., Schmidt, P., Shim, Y., 1992. Testing the null hypothesis of stationarity against the alternative of a unit root: how sure are we that economic time series are non-stationary? Journal of Econometrics 54 (1—3), 159—178.

Lamoureux, C., Lastrapes, W., 1990. Persistence in variance, structural change, and the GARCH model. Journal of Business and Economic Statistics 8 (2), 225—234.

Li, Y., Giles, D. E., 2015. Modelling volatility spillover effects between developed stock markets and Asian emerging stock markets. International Journal of Finance & Economics 20, 155—177.

Ljung, G. M., Box, G. E. P., 1978. On a measure of lack of fit in Time Series Models. Biometrika 65 (2), 297—303.

Markowitz, H., 1952. Portfolio selection. Journal of Finance 7 (1), 77—91.

Marr, J., Reynard, C., 2010. Investing in emerging markets: the BRIC economies and beyond. Wiley Online Library.

Masih, A. M. M., Masih, R., 1999. Are Asian stock market fluctuations due mainly to intra-regional contagion effects? evidence based on Asian emerging stock markets. Pacific-Basin Finance Journal 7, 251—282.

Mensi, W., Hammoudeh, S., Kang, S. H., 2015a. Precious metals, cereal, oil and stock market linkages and portfolio risk management: evidence from Saudi Arabia. Economic Modelling 51, 340—358.

Mensi, W., Hammoudeh, S., Kang, S. H., 2017. Risk spillovers and portfolio management between developed and BRICS stock markets. North American Journal of Economics and Finance 41, 133—155.

Mensi, W., Hammoudeh, S., Yoon, S.-M., 2015b. Structural breaks, dynamic correlations, asymmetric volatility transmission, and hedging strategies for petroleum prices and USD exchange rate. Energy Economics 48, 46—60.

Mollah, S., Quoreshi, A. M. M. S., Zafirov, G., 2016. Equity market contagion during global financial and eurozone crises: evidence from a dynamic correlation analysis. Journal of International Financial Markets, Institutions & Money 41, 151—167.

Narayan, P. K., Sharma, S. S., 2015. Does data frequency matter for the impact of forward premium on spot exchange rate? International Review of Financial Analysis 39, 45—53.

Nelson, D. B., 1991. Conditional heteroscedasticity in asset returns: a new approach. Econometrica 59, 347—370.

Philips, P. C. B., Perron, P., 1988. Testing for unit roots in time series regression. Biometrika 75 (2), 335—346.

Ramasamy, B., Yeung, M., Laforet, S., 2012. China's outward foreign direct investment: location choice and firm ownership. Journal of World Business 47, 17—25.

Robinson, P. M., Henry, M., 1999. Long and short memory conditional heteroscedasticity in estimating the memory parameter of levels. Econometric Theory 15 (3), 299—336.

Shen, Y., 2018. International risk transmission of stock market movements. Economic Modelling 69, 220—236.

UNCTAD, 2017. World investment report 2017. Geneva, UN Publications.

Wang, P., Moore, T., 2009. Sudden changes in volatility: the case of five central European stock markets. Journal of International Financial Markets, Institutions and Money 19 (1), 33—46.

Wu, P., Shieh, S. J., 2007. Value-at-risk analysis for long-term interest rate futures: fat-tail and long memory in return innovations. Journal of Empirical Finance 14 (2), 248—259.

Zhang, X., Daly, K., 2011. The determinants of China's outward foreign direct investment. Emerging Markets Review 12, 389—398.

Chapter 4

Aloui, C., Hkiri, B., 2014. Co-movements of GCC emerging stock markets: new evidence from wavelet coherence analysis. Economic Modelling 36, 421—431.

Baker, M., Stein, J. C., 2004. Market liquidity as a sentiment indicator. Journal of Financial Markets 7 (3), 271—299.

Baker, M., Wurgler, J., 2006. Investor sentiment and the cross-section of stock returns. Journal of Finance 61, 1645—1680.

Balli, F., Hajhoj, H. R., Basherd, S. A., Ghassan, H. B., 2015. An analysis of returns and volatility spillovers and their determinants in emerging Asian and Middle Eastern countries. International Review of Economics and Finance 39, 311—325.

Baur, D. G., 2013. The structure and degree of dependence: a quantile regression approach. Journal of Banking & Finance 37, 786—798.

Baur, D. G., Dimpfl, T., Jung, R. C., 2012. Stock return autocorrelations revisited: a quantile regression approach. Journal of Empirical Finance 19, 254—265.

Baur, D. G., Lucey, B., 2010. Is gold a hedge or safe haven? An analysis of stocks bonds and gold. Financial Review 45 (2), 217—229.

Baur, D. G., McDermott, T., 2010. Is gold a safe haven? International evidence. Journal of Banking & Finance 34, 1886—1898.

Bekaert, G., Harvey, C. R., 1995. Time-varying world market integration. Journal of Finance 50, 403—444.

Borah, B. J., Basu, A., 2013. Highlighting differences between conditional and unconditional quantile regression approaches through an application to assess medication adherence. Health Economics 22, 1052—1070.

Chau, F., Deesomsak, R., Koutmos, D., 2016. Does investor sentiment really matter? International Review of Financial Analysis 48, 221—232.

Chen, P. , Semmler, W. , 2018. Financial stress, regime switching and spillover effects: evidence from a multi-regime global VAR model. Journal of Economic Dynamics & Control 91, 318—348.

Chen, Q. , Lv, X. , 2015. The extreme-value dependence between the crude oil price and Chinese stock markets. International Review of Economics and Finance 39, 121—132.

Chudik, A. , Fratzscher, M. , 2011. Identifying the global transmission of the 2007—2009 financial crisis in a GVAR model. European Economic Review 55, 325—339.

Cotter, J. , Hanly, J. , 2012. Hedging effectiveness under conditions of asymmetry. European Journal of Finance 18 (2), 135—147.

Dickey, D. A. , Fuller, W. , 1979. Distribution of the estimators for autoregressive time series with a unit root. Journal of the American Statistical Association 74 (336), 427—431.

Dimitriou, D. , Kenourgios, D. , Simos, T. , 2013. Global financial crisis and emerging stock market contagion: a multivariate FIAPARCH – DCC approach. International Review of Financial Analysis 30, 46—56.

Fama, E. F. , 1970. Efficient capital markets: a review of theory and empirical work. Journal of Finance 25 (2), 383—417.

Fama, E. F. , 1998. Market efficiency, long-term returns, and behavioral finance. Journal of Financial Economics 49 (3), 283—306.

Firpo, S. , Fortin, N. M. , Lemieux, T. , 2009. Unconditional quantile regression. Econometrica 77 (3), 953—973.

Guesmi, K. , Nguyen, D. K. , 2011. How strong is the global integration of emerging market regions? An empirical assessment. Economic Modelling 28, 2517—2527.

Guidi, F. , Ugur, M. , 2014. An analysis of South-Eastern

European stock markets: evidence on cointegration and portfolio diversification benefits. Journal of International Financial Markets, Institutions & Money 30, 119—136.

Hampel, F. R., Ronchetti, E. M., Rousseeuw, P. J., Stahel, W. A., 2005. Robust statistics: the approach based on influence functions. Wiley, New York.

Jansen, D. W., Tsai, C. -L., 2010. Monetary policy and stock returns: Financing constraints and asymmetries in bull and bear markets. Journal of Empirical Finance 17, 981—990.

Jareño, F., Ferrer, R., Miroslavova, S., 2016. US stock market sensitivity to interest and inflation rates: a quantile regression approach. Applied Economics 48 (26), 2469—2481.

Jarque, C. M., Bera, A. K., 1980. Efficient tests for normality, homoscedasticity and serial independence of regression residuals. Economic Letters 6 (3), 255—259.

Johansson, A. C., Ljungwall, C., 2009. Spillover effects among the Greater China stock markets. World Development 37 (4), 839—851.

Kenourgios, D., Dimitriou, D., 2015. Contagion of the Global Financial Crisis and the real economy: a regional analysis. Economic Modelling 44, 283—293.

Kocaarslan, B., Sari, R., Gormus, A., Soytas, U., 2017. Dynamic correlations between BRIC and U. S. stock markets: the asymmetric impact of volatility expectations in oil, gold and financial markets. Journal of Commodity Markets 7, 41—56.

Koenker, R. W., 2005. Quantile regression. Cambridge University Press, New York.

Koenker, R. W., Bassett, G., 1978. Regression quantiles. Econometrica 46 (1), 33—50.

Koenker, R. W., D'Orey, V., 1987. Computing regression quantiles. Applied Statistics 36, 383—393.

Kumar, A., Lee, C. M., 2006. Retail investor sentiment and return comovements. Journal of Finance 61, 2451—2486.

Kwiatkowski, D., Phillips, P. C. B., Schmidt, P., Shim, Y., 1992. Testing the null hypothesis of stationarity against the alternative of a unit root: how sure are we that economic time series are non-stationary? Journal of Econometrics 54 (1—3), 159—178.

Laopodis, N. T., 2013. Monetary policy and stock market dynamics across monetary regimes. Journal of International Money and Finance 33, 381—406.

Li, J., 2015. The asymmetric effects of investor sentiment and monetary policy on stock prices. Applied Economics 47 (24), 2514—2522.

Markowitz, H., 1952. Portfolio selection. Journal of Finance 7 (1), 77—91.

Mensi, W., Hammoudeh, S., Kang, S. H., 2017. Risk spillovers and portfolio management between developed and BRICS stock markets. North American Journal of Economics and Finance 41, 133—155.

Mensi, W., Hammoudeh, S., Reboredo, J. C., Nguyen, D. K., 2014. Do global factors impact BRICS stock markets? A quantile regression approach. Emerging Markets Review 19, 1—17.

Mishra, A. K., Mottaleb, K. A., Mohanty, S., 2015. Impact of off-farm income on food expenditures in rural Bangladesh: an unconditional quantile regression approach. Agricultural Economics 46, 139—148.

Ni, Z.-X., Wang, D.-Z., Xue, W.-J., 2015. Investor sentiment and its nonlinear effect on stock returns—new evidence from the Chinese stock market based on panel quantile regression model. Economic Modelling 50, 266—274.

Philips, P. C. B., Perron, P., 1988. Testing for unit roots in time series regression. Biometrika 75 (2), 335—346.

Reboredo, J. C., Uddin, G. S., 2016. Do financial stress and policy uncertainty have an impact on the energy and metals markets? A quantile regression approach. International Review of Economics and Finance 43, 284—298.

Reboredo, J. C., Ugolini, A., 2016. Quantile dependence of oil price movements and stock returns. Energy Economics 54, 33—49.

Shiller, R. J., 2015. Irrational exuberance. Princeton University Press, Princeton, New Jersey.

Sortino, F. A., van der Meer, R., 1991. Downside risk. Journal of Portfolio Management 17 (4), 27—31.

Tsai, I. -C., 2012. The relationship between stock price index and exchange rate in Asian markets: a quantile regression approach. Journal of International Financial Markets, Institutions & Money 22, 609—621.

Yang, C., Li, J., 2013. Investor sentiment, information and asset pricing model. Economic Modelling 35, 436—442.

Yang, C., Li, J., 2014. Two-period trading sentiment asset pricing model with information. Economic Modelling 36, 1—7.

You, W., Guo. Y., Zhu, H., Tang, Y., 2017. Oil price shocks, economic policy uncertainty and industry stock returns in China: asymmetric effects with quantile regression. Energy Economics 68, 1—18.

This book is the result of a co-publication agreement between China Financial and Economic Publishing House (China) and Paths International Ltd (UK).

Title: The Global Stock Market Nexus Considering External Factors
Author: Dong Xiyong
ISBN: 978-1-84464-730-9
Ebook ISBN: 978-1-84464-731-6

Paths International Ltd

Published in the United Kingdom
www.pathsinternational.com

www.ingramcontent.com/pod-product-compliance
Lightning Source LLC
LaVergne TN
LVHW081208240426
836338LV00004B/41